Abstract

Religion is a topic that businesses often ignore, in spite of 70% of the world being religious. Whether the silence results from the taboo nature of the topic or the thought that religion is a separate domain from consumption and business, it cannot be denied that it has received scant attention. Many do not realize (or resist) the idea that religion is a key contributor to a consumer's core values, which then contribute to consumption decisions, voting practices, reaction to pro-social messages and public policy, as well as donating behavior.

The field of behavioral economics discusses how various social and cognitive factors influence economic decisions, which encompass consumer decision making. This field needs to incorporate religion as an influence on economic decision making. To be able to manage a business effectively, to market to consumers of various religious backgrounds properly and effectively, to develop public policy acceptable across religious boundaries, and to interact with other business professionals, an understanding of religion and business is, and will continue to be, especially important in the business world.

Thus, this book provides one of the first comprehensive investigations into the relationship between religion and behavioral economics. We discuss the importance of religion in the field of business along with managerial implications in great detail. The basic premises of the major religious affiliations (Christianity, Judaism, Islam, Hinduism, Buddhism, and Confucianism/Taoism) are reviewed. We bring to life prior research on religion and behavioral economics with an emphasis on how this research can help practitioners to improve business practices.

In this book, we look at how religion relates to consumer behavior from a scientific perspective. We try to observe and understand the consequences of very real beliefs. We critique our efforts from the point of view of epistemology, not hermeneutics. We will leave to others with different training and knowledge the quest for religious Truth, but we respect people who sincerely and honestly search for either scientific truth, religious Truth, or both.

This book is relevant to current managers, anyone involved in marketing, MBA students, and also upper-division undergraduate students. Each of these groups will benefit from a clear understanding of religious groups and the influence of religion on consumer decision making. Readers of this book will learn to create marketing campaigns inclusive of all religious affiliations or directed toward specific religious affiliations, to interact with business associates with different religious beliefs, and to develop public policy or pro-social messages aimed at approval from certain religious groups.

Keywords

religion, religiosity, religious affiliation, belief systems, Christian, Jew, Muslim, Hindu, Buddhist, Confucianist, Taoist, behavioral economics, consumer behavior, decision making, morality, donation behavior, sustainability, holidays

Contents

Preface

We are pleased to introduce our book on religion, belief systems, and behavioral economics. Across all fields of business, religion is often seen as a taboo topic. We have found when presenting religion and consumer behavior papers that academic audience members often either protest that religion has no part in business or want to proselytize for their own religious beliefs; however, religion has a definite (and non-proselytizing) place in business and, more specifically, in behavioral economics. We know how critical it is when studying such a controversial topic to take a scientific vantage point – we are not advocating faith but rather scientifically examining how faith influences many different aspects of consumption, consumer-related decision making, and behavioral economics. At the same time, we have respect for people who seek religious Truth, scientific truth, or both.

The target for this book is threefold:

- First, it's for businesses that desire to understand target markets more effectively, design better product offerings, and improve their understanding of religious influences on marketing efforts.
- Second, it's for classes and students studying culture and behavioral economics, international marketing, or any other course examining the influences of religion, culture, or international markets on business.
- Third, it's for academics across a variety of fields (e.g., behavioral economics, marketing, religion) as a thorough review of literature on the topic of religion and behavioral economics providing an insight into gaps in the research that need to be explored further.

The topic for this book emerged from a mutual interest in consumer values. One of the authors (lk) developed the List of Values, which is a measurement instrument for understanding a consumer's core values. Out of this research tradition, we both asked the question—what determines a consumer's core values? One part of the answer was "religion." Throughout this book, we discuss how religion pervades society both for people who are religious and people who are not. Additionally, we describe how those that do not believe in a God (i.e., atheists) and those who are uncertain about the existence of God (i.e., agnostics) also carry a belief system that influences behavioral economics. Because of this important relation between belief systems and consumption and the lack of prior research in the area, we decided to write this book. We hope you find the book as interesting to read as we have found researching the topic and writing the book.

We, two marketing scholars, wrote this book for a series in behavioral economics. Marketing has two academic parent disciplines—economics, which believes that people are always rational and behave in their self-interest, and psychology, which believes that people are never rational and frequently behave in an inexplicable manner. Perhaps the topic of religion, more than any other, taunts both parent disciplines—behavioral economics and consumer psychology—because intellectually it disobeys the rules of both. Yet the importance of religion in many people's daily lives is an empirical fact awaiting explication or punishment for breaking all the rules. Our challenge in this book was to tackle the illusive running back of an idea that is rather impressive in its run across the field. We hope through this discussion to set the stage for further discussion about the bases of both behavioral economics and consumer psychology.

The timing of this book is perhaps in part a result of the emergence of "Big Data" access and analysis techniques. Religion is highly complex, and many of the attempts to study it have fallen short of optimal potential because of simplistic approaches. With the growth of Big Data, it is now possible to model religion's effects in a much more complex manner than was previously possible. Thus, the time seems ripe to examine the complexity of religion in relation to behavioral economics.

Of course, the completion of this book could not have been possible without the help of many people. We are immensely thankful to Dr. Norm Metzler, for his detailed and theologically insightful comments on and improvements to our book. We appreciate our many friends from various belief traditions who provided insights into their worlds. We would also like to thank Dr. Philip Romero for his encouragement to write this book as well as many others at Business Expert Press, including Dr. Jeff Edwards, who have helped along the way in the publication process. Of course, we cannot end our list of thanks without giving credit to our spouses, Dr. Debra Eisert and Daniel Minton, who have put in many hours editing our work, being a sounding board for ideas, and being supportive all through the process.

Whether you are a manager, academic, or student, we hope this book will inspire you to think about the relationship between religion and consumption and to integrate this newfound perspective into the work that you do.

CHAPTER 1

Behavioral Economics and Belief Systems

Introduction

Religion is a topic that businesses often ignore, in spite of 70% of the world being religious. Whether the silence results from the taboo nature of the topic or the thought that religion is a separate domain from consumption and business, it cannot be denied that it has received scant attention. Many resist the idea (or do not realize) that religion is a key contributor to a consumer's core values, which then contribute to consumption decisions, voting practices, reaction to pro-social messages and public policy, as well as donating behavior. All cultures have a concept of God and of spirituality, although definitions and acceptance of those concepts vary.

The field of behavioral economics discusses how various social and cognitive factors influence economic decisions, which encompass consumer decision making. This field needs to incorporate belief systems (a primary one of which is religion) as an influence on economic decision making. To be able to manage a business effectively, to market to consumers of various religious backgrounds, to develop public policy acceptable across religious boundaries, and to interact with other business professionals, an understanding of religion and business is, and will continue to be, especially important in the business world.

Thus, this book provides one of the first comprehensive investigations into the relation between religion and behavioral economics. The chapters of the book explore the importance of religion in the field of business along with managerial implications. The basic premises of the major religious affiliations (Christianity, Judaism, Islam, Hinduism, Buddhism, and Confucianism/Taoism) are reviewed. More specifically, the chapters to follow bring to life prior research on religion and behavioral economics with an emphasis on how this research can help practitioners to improve business practices.

Advances in data collection in our current age of Big Data have led to new avenues for collecting consumer data on religion and belief systems.[1] Consumer data are everywhere today—within social media, on store loyalty cards, in corporate databases. These data provide unique insights into consumer religious profiles that are often lying dormant waiting for businesses to use them to improve marketing practices. A mixture of Big Data and social media (where consumers can self-select into religious groups) are leading to a new age of marketing that is pivotal to the field of behavioral economics.

Behavioral Economics Versus Marketing

The field of behavioral economics dates back to the 1700s.[2] This field studies how social-cognitive biases influence the economy through market prices, supply and demand, and consumer behavior. Behavioral economics is well known especially for three areas: (1) framing (e.g., an advertisement framed as gaining $50 for purchasing an energy efficient appliance vs. losing $50 for not purchasing the appliance), (2) heuristics (i.e., mental shortcuts humans use to make decisions, such as seeing two options and assuming the more expensive one is higher quality), and (3) market inefficiencies (i.e., incorporating human behavioral explanations for why rational economic models do not always work).

The field of marketing began to takeoff with the beginning of the industrial revolution in the 1800s.[3] Marketing extends the field of behavioral economics to focus more on providing value to the consumer in addition to exploring strategies for effective execution of methods for selling products, services, people, or ideas that can be used by companies and policy makers alike. Contemporary marketing is not just about selling products but also about providing value to the consumer and even involves developing public policy to protect consumers from harmful behaviors. Good marketing typically begins by finding out what consumers want before developing products or attempting to sell them profitably. It is much easier to "sell" something if the potential customer wants it. Thus, behavioral economics examines human behavior in relation to economic changes whereas marketing explores economic and corporate behavior in relation to both economic and non-economic (e.g., satisfaction) changes. In practice the two fields often overlap in topics of interest.

In behavioral economics, scholars use the results of psychological and economic experiments to evaluate the predictive power of core assumptions about the behavior of economic actors. They choose options according to economic theory based on their net benefits, make resource decisions at the margin, or maximize personal utility. The core of economics retains the assumption that individuals are mostly motivated by self-interest. Many religions direct adherents to act in ways that are inimical to short-term self-interest, by exalting a deity or by showing charity. These actions are, of course, mostly contrary to traditional microeconomic behavioral assumptions, which continue to influence behavioral economics. This entire book illustrates the implications of such belief systems, but it does not advance our belief in the rational decision making of humans. Indeed, it may bring cold water to the party by providing an extended counterexample, although in some cases religion may push people to behave more rationally (e.g., in promoting health). We hope this book inspires further conversation about behavioral economic theory even as it expands into new terrain, but we do not dwell on behavioral economic theory as we review our evidence.

Why Religion?

Religion is everywhere, and for many people it represents the backbone of everyday behavior. Why then has so little research been conducted on assessing how religion influences consumer behavior? Almost every study highlights the exploratory nature of the relation between religion and consumption, and there are virtually no attempts to replicate religion and consumer behavior studies. Whether it is the taboo nature of religion or the fact that academics are more focused on the hot topics in other domains, the field of behavioral economics is missing a significant component of consumer behavior. Before delving into the few studies that have examined the relation between religion and consumer behavior, we will attempt to provide a clear understanding of religion.

In the United States, almost 50% of all people over the age of 18 attend church more than once a month.[4] Over one-quarter (25.4%) of Americans attend church at least every week.[5] More than 50% of Americans self-report praying at least once per day, with 27.4% reportedly praying several times per day.[6] Americans are highly religious. About 62% express confidence that God exists, 82% are at least somewhat confident that God exists, and 60% are at least moderately religious according to a study on consumers' self-reported religiosity.[7] Important to business managers and academics alike is that 70.7% of Americans carry their religious beliefs into other aspects of life (e.g., shopping).[8] Only 16.1% of Americans are completely unaffiliated with any religious belief, which includes both agnostics and atheists.[9] Even for agnostics and atheists, their uncertainty or belief that God does not exist actually represents a belief system that then influences many choices they make, including consumer choices.

Understanding household religious affiliation is no longer satisfactory because 37% of Americans have spouses of different religious affiliations.[10] Knowing the religious affiliation of the primary shopper and decision maker in the household can clue businesses in to the appropriate products and services to target at these consumers, such as providing a better understanding of how to market products during the Christmas and Hanukkah holiday season (a religious season that can represent anywhere from 20%–40% of many retail companies' yearly sales).[11] However, a complete understanding of the implications of religion requires an individual-level inquiry.

Religion and Science

Religion and science are sometimes viewed as being at odds, with some people reluctant to discuss religion because it is not "scientific." Both religion and science are searching for knowledge, but each uses different rules and has different goals. It is important to understand the differences between the two systems with both being vital to the understanding of human nature.

Science seeks truth with a small "t." For something to be true scientifically, it must be observable. What we can observe, of course, changes with time. Thus, improved observation methods, such as better tele-scopes, microscopes, or x-ray machines, change what we can observe and therefore change science. Every good scientist should willingly change views appropriately when new things are observed or new methods of observation render prior "truths" obsolete. This principle applies both to the natural sciences and to the social sciences. Science wants knowledge that meets certain criteria, such as usefulness and prediction. Individual scientists may have varied motives, such as helping humanity or solving vexing problems. Epistemology is the branch of philosophy/science that explores these rules of establishing scientific truths. This field is, of course, more complex and detailed than our one-paragraph summary reveals.

Religion, on the other hand, uses faith and sacred texts rather than observation in its search for Truth, and the Truth it seeks is spelled with a capital "T." Religion seeks eternal wisdom and does not rely exclusively on current observational knowledge. Religions want knowledge that will guide humanity in understanding its most fundamental eternal, exis-tential, and ethical questions. Individual theologians may have varied motives, such as helping humanity or solving vexing problems. Herme-neutics is the branch of philosophy/theology that explores these rules of establishing religious Truths. Similar to science, the field of religion is, of course, more complex and detailed than our one-paragraph summary reveals.

Every good scientist will acknowledge that many real phenomena defy observational knowledge and yet influence us in spite of our current observational capacities. Every good theologian will acknowledge that sci-ence has contributed much to humanity's well-being. Additionally, we all acknowledge that we have faith in certain things we do not completely understand, such as power transmission or the postal service. The search for truth and Truth have different standards, different methods, and dif-ferent goals. When each is used and understood properly, the two do not necessarily have to be at war, and both can contribute significantly to our understanding of human behavior. There are many examples of religious scientists and scientific religious leaders. Very often conflicts arise when the principles of hermeneutics are inappropriately applied to science or the principles of epistemology are inappropriately applied to theology. Imagine someone who knows that microscopes enhance observational searching and that eating oranges can enhance health. Applying the principles and techniques of microscopy would almost certainly not help a hungry person desiring oranges find an orange grove.

In this book, we look at how religion relates to consumer behavior from a scientific perspective. We try to observe and understand the consequences of very real beliefs. We critique our efforts from the point of view of epistemology, not hermeneutics. We will leave to others with different training and knowledge the quest for religious Truth, but we respect people who sincerely and honestly search for truth, Truth, or both.

Behavioral Economics and Belief Systems

Religion guides traditions of beliefs, values, and economic behavior even among people who do not consider themselves faithful. For example, Karl Marx, an atheist, was trained and baptized as a Lutheran and was the grandson of a Dutch rabbi.[12] Although he explicitly rejected religion, his economic theories bear a striking resemblance to the philosophy espoused in the New Testament (see, e.g., Acts 2). Many of the moral and normative beliefs common in Judeo-Christian traditions, such as honesty or opposition to homicide, guide social interaction well beyond the religious community. When dealing with uncertain social demands, tradition can exert a strong influence. Sherif showed that the autokinetic illusion, the illusory movement of light against a black background, can be judged to move a greater distance by having another person (i.e., a confederate) state with confidence how great the "movement" of the light is. If one person tells a real subject that the light "moves" a greater distance than expected, then the real subject tends to repeat this to the next ("new generation") subject as a sincere judgment, and the second judgment is also inflated.[13] This judgment inflation can persist for many generations in spite of no supporting evidence of the judgment.

Likewise, normative behavior from religion influences people for many generations, even when they reject the founding basis. For example, St. Thomas Aquinas supported the concept of just pricing, which reflects the idea that value should be traded for equivalent value (e.g., a product for its equivalent value in money) that stems from the Biblical idea of treating others with respect and fairness.[14] Although this idea has been morphed to reflect new interpretations of value, the same principle still influences society today—product pricing should reflect product value for consumers to purchase the product. Moreover, with religion, the founding basis often persists. For example, on a recent tour of St. Peter's church in Vienna, Austria, one of us was told that people had celebrated mass at that location every day consecutively for more than a thousand years. That tradition nearly defines persistence.

Of course, the relation between beliefs and behaviors is never simple. A striking strategy for a social science researcher is to demonstrate hypocrisy, and showing religious hypocrisy may be one of the easier places to succeed with this strategy. Yet the displays of hypocrisy attract attention precisely because they are counterintuitive. The relations between attitudes and behaviors are always complicated, and certainly religious behaviors do not always flow simply and directly from simple beliefs. Yet one must wonder when observing inconsistent behaviors how representative of all behaviors those examples are. Researchers specializing in hypocrisy rarely draw large, representative samples of behavior. Sweeping generalizations about the relation between religious attitudes and religious behaviors should examine both the attitudes and the behaviors reliably in their full complexity. At the very least this topic is worthy of further research.

CHAPTER 2

Demystifying Belief Systems

In this chapter, the concept of a belief system is explored from the point of view that a consumer's core beliefs lead to purchase behavior. A popular methodological example of this perspective is means-end chain analysis, in which the core values associated with a behavior are derived.[1] In this type of analysis, a researcher first asks the consumer why he or she purchased a product. Take a tube of toothpaste as an example. The researcher would ask, "Why did you purchase this brand of toothpaste?" The consumer typically responds with an attribute of the toothpaste, for example, "It contains fluoride." The researcher would then continue to ask why this reason is important—"Why is it important for you to brush your teeth with fluoride?" The consumer then typically responds with another reason—"I care about my health." The researcher would then continue to explore the core belief behind this reason—"Why do you care about your health?" The consumer typically provides an explanation associated with his or her belief system—"I want to care for the body that God gave me" might be a response. This sequence completes the means-end chain analysis that explores why a consumer makes a purchase, revealing that core beliefs and values drive consumer choices. Thus, understanding a consumer's core beliefs and values reveals the underlying reason in a consumer deciding what to purchase. This value-driven decision is the building block of all economic behavior. Religious views provide guidance for many consumers in developing these values.[2]

Belief Systems

Belief systems represent the core values that drive everyday behavior. These core values (e.g., sense of accomplishment, warm relationships with others, fun and enjoyment in life) can effectively describe consumer decision making, especially among highly involved purchase decisions.[3] The Merriam-Webster dictionary defines belief as "Conviction of the truth of some statement or the reality of some being or phenomenon especially when based on examination of evidence."[4] This conviction of the truth represents a core value of a consumer.

To define belief systems, one must ask where a consumer obtains his or her core beliefs. The answer to this question lies in either religion or other teaching sources (e.g., family members, schooling, cultural standards). However, teasing apart these two sources of core beliefs is nearly impossible because of the fact that many laws and cultural standards were first based on religious values. Thus, *belief systems* are a composition of values that are derived from religious doctrine, cultural standards, and teaching in schools and by mentors. These values represent the consumer's beliefs on the importance of family, the need for self-success and money, the desire for fun and enjoyment in life, the role of relationships with others in daily life, and the necessity of moral behavior, among others. Together, these values define a belief system that can then be used to understand a consumer's behavior in the marketplace.

Although religion represents one of the most important core belief systems of consumers today, many alternative belief systems may also motivate consumers. For example, consumers who do not believe in religion (i.e., atheists) still have a belief system that can be understood as opposition to religious belief systems (i.e., believing that God does not exist). Because a belief is defined as "conviction of the truth," an atheist holds a belief that God does not exist, and therefore this view influences attitudes and behaviors. Agnostics view religious Truth as unknowable. This position follows the popular phrase from Harvey Cox, "not to decide is to decide." The atheistic movement now features consumer products with the letter "A" to represent atheism in addition to atheistic summer camps for children that emphasize evolution.[5] These are just a sampling of ways in which atheism influences consumption.

As another example, some consumers see themselves as naturalists and worship nature. This worship of nature is not necessarily believing that nature has a spirit but rather that nature is to be worshipped for its beauty and cared for because it can be easily destroyed. In a sense, this natural belief system guides consumer behavior as these consumers try to avoid any products or services that would harm the environment and instead make choices as to how to give back and care for the environment. These are just a sampling of alternative belief systems that are rooted in core values and describe why consumers make the decisions they do.

Religion as a Belief System

A consumer's religious affiliation is one of the main sources of core values that define a belief system. Both religious scriptures and teachings of current-day religious leaders provide guidance for many people about what is important in life and about how to handle life's tough situations. Religions provide guidance on many topics, including the idea of worshipping God before other things (e.g., money, relationships, material objects), caring for others like oneself, and respecting the environment. Each of these guidelines builds the foundation of a belief system, which then influences other decisions such as purchase behavior. Because almost all religions emphasize the need to obey God or the spirit above and beyond any physical objects or material desires on earth, core religious values provide important belief systems for religious adherents and an interesting area of analysis for businesses.

Defining Religion

There is no all-encompassing definition of religion.[6] Instead, the definition of *religion* is often adjusted based upon the context of the discussion or the purpose of the research study.[7] Defining religion even for a particular context is difficult because the definition must encompass monotheistic (believing in one god) and polytheistic religions (believing in multiple gods) in addition to religions that do not believe in a God (e.g., the Buddhist's search for spiritual enlightenment or the Confucianist's beliefs in the moral teachings of Confucius).[8] Religion is composed of two main parts: (1) religiosity—the degree or intensity of belief and (2) religious affiliation—the actual belief system.

Religiosity

In contrast to religion, which represents a belief system, religiosity represents how strongly a person holds these beliefs. In other words, religion

represents the "what" of beliefs (i.e., what do you believe?), and religiosity represents the "how" of beliefs (i.e., how strongly do you believe?).
Delener defines religiosity as "the degree to which beliefs in specific
religious values and ideals are held and practiced by an individual."[9]
Religious involvement, often synonymous with religiosity, is defined by
Himmelfarb as "the degree to which a person's religion occupies his or her
interests, beliefs, or activities.[10] However, Wilkes, Burnett, and Howell
note that there are as many different definitions for religiosity as there are
authors.[11]

Religiosity levels range from non-believers to associates ("I associated
myself with the religion, but I do not believe any of its core tenets") to
casual believers ("I believe what I want") to strong believers ("I believe
all the tenets and frequently practice my beliefs"). Non-believers fall
into one of two categories—atheists or agnostics. Although this book
focuses on religious belief systems, it is still important to acknowledge
that non-believers are grouped together by a belief system of disbelief
(i.e., they agree that they do not believe in religion). While atheists do not
believe in any God or spiritual power, agnostics argue that it is impossible
to know if a God exists and therefore do not worship any God.

For religious believers, Allport and Ross distinguish between intrinsic (e.g., spirituality) and extrinsic (e.g., church attendance) religiosity.[12]
Often, intrinsic religiosity is seen as the more pure and true religiosity
because it is not done as a means of identity expression (i.e., let me show
you how religious a person I am). Acts of intrinsic religiosity include personal prayer and meditation, strength of personal relationship with God
or spirit, and use of the God or spirit to guide decisions and behaviors.

Extrinsic religiosity, on the other hand, includes activities that
are public and seen by others. This category includes activities such as
church attendance, wearing religious jewelry, having religious bumper
stickers, religious postings on social media outlets, or hosting religious
get-togethers. Extrinsic religiosity can be considered similar to conspicu-
ous consumption where an act of religiousness could be done merely for
show (though not always). Any definition of religiosity should address
both the intrinsic and extrinsic nature of religiosity. Therefore, for the
purposes of this book, *religiosity* is defined as *the degree to which one holds*

religious beliefs and values both through an internal spiritual connection and external religious practices and behaviors.

Religious Affiliation

The word *religion* is based on its Latin root *religio,* which represents a connection between humanity and a power greater than that of humans.[13] One of the first definitions of religion comes from Lenski and applies to more than just theistic faiths (i.e., faiths based on a single god or multiple gods): "a system of beliefs about the nature of the force(s) ultimately shaping man's destiny, and the practices associated therewith, shared by the members of a group."[14] Religious definitions are also classified very simply such as Kale's definition of "a road map for spirituality."[15]

Recent religious definitions attempt to conceptualize the differences between religion and spirituality,[16] often finding that religion encompasses more institutional formalities in contrast to spirituality that encompasses more intangible aspects.[17] However, definitions for both religion and spirituality are diverse. Hill and colleagues define spirituality as "the feelings, thoughts, experiences, and behaviors that arise from a search for the sacred."[18] Kale defines spirituality as an "engagement to explore—and deeply and meaningfully connect one's inner self—to the known world and Beyond."[19] Religion encompasses spirituality, institutional rituals and behaviors, and "a search for non-sacred goals" (e.g., identity, belongingness, meaning, and health).[20] Although not exclusively, spirituality more often refers to the intrinsic aspects of religion, and religious affiliation captures both intrinsic and extrinsic aspects of religion. However, spirituality and religion are being merged and molded to develop new varieties of religious beliefs (e.g., religious pluralism), which Charles Taylor describes in his award winning book, *Secular Age,* as the current great transitory time for the Western world.[21] As Taylor posits, support for humanism (i.e., individual thought greater than faith) may be increasing, but the desire for fullness and meaning provided by religion and spirituality also continues which then influences human behavior.

In another definition, Bowker defines *religion* as views that "bind people together in common practices and beliefs... in a common goal of life."[22] However, this definition lacks the incorporation of a higher spiritual or godly being. Yet, this definition does provide insight into how religion can greatly influence consumer behavior. The social networks of religious institutions can become a consumer's core group of friends that includes opinion leaders who guide decisions in the marketplace. If this group of people forbids or discourages certain products or services, demand for these products and services will decrease. If this group instead encourages other products or services, demand for these products or services will increase. With the strong emphasis on trust and truthfulness in most religions, opinions and behaviors in these groups (i.e., word of mouth communication) can weigh much more strongly than those of nonexperts outside the group. As is often said in business, word of mouth is one of the most effective forms of marketing communication.

Based on the wide variety of definitions for religion and spirituality, these two terms will be defined separately for our purpose, to apply these definitions to all world religions. *Religious affiliation* represents *a commonly held set of beliefs and values that guide external behavior and an internal search for meaning and may include institutional practices such as religious services or religious social networks.* In contrast, spirituality represents *an internal search for meaning in life that is often encompassed in a religion.*

It is important for studies to address more than just religious affiliation because a person could identify with a religion but follow none of its beliefs. In America, Christians in this category are often known as "Casual Christians," "C&E Christians," or "Sunday Christians." The C and E in C&E Christians refer to Christmas and Easter, because these casual Christians only go to religious services on the two biggest Christian holidays of the year. Sunday Christians receive their name because they attend religious services on Sunday but do not necessarily do anything throughout the week to practice the faith. Oftentimes, the Sunday Christians are exclusively extrinsically religious, meaning that they go to church on Sunday to appear religious but do nothing internally to practice the religion. Therefore, a combined measure of religion and religiosity is important for an accurate assessment of how religion affects consumer behavior.[23] See Table 2.1 for a summary of definitions of terms that are used throughout this book.

Table 2.1. Religion Definitions

Belief system	Composition of values that are derived from religious doctrine, cultural standards, and teaching in schools and by mentors
Religion	Composed of two parts: (1) religiosity and (2) religious affiliation
Religiosity	Degree to which one holds religious beliefs and values both through an internal spiritual connection and external religious practice and behavior
Religious associate	"I associate myself with the religion, but I do not believe any of its core tenets"
Casual believer	"I believe what I want"
Strong believer	"I believe all tenets and frequently practice my beliefs"
Agnostic	Believes that it is not possible to know whether God (or other divine being) exists
Atheist	Believes that God (or other divine being) does not exist
Intrinsic religiosity	An internal, spiritual connection with God (e.g., personal prayer)
Extrinsic religiosity	An external connection with sacraments and other visual forms of religious adherence (e.g., church attendance)
Religious affiliation	A commonly held set of beliefs and values that guide external behavior and an internal search for meaning and may include institutional practices such as religious services or religious social networks
Spirituality	An internal search for meaning in life that is often encompassed within religion

Measuring Belief Systems

In order for religion to be useful to businesses, it is important to know how to measure both aspects of religion—religiosity and religious affiliation. Both of these constructs provide insights into a consumer's core values, belief systems, and, ultimately, purchase related behavior.

Religiosity

Numerous studies have found that religiosity is a multidimensional construct.[24] Spirituality, a component of religiosity, is also a multidimensional construct[25] and has been measured using the multidimensional spiritual transcendence scale[26] and spiritual transcendence index.[27] Therefore, simply asking a person to state his or her perceived level of religiosity is not adequate to capture all aspects of religiosity fully.[28] For example, if you ask a consumer, "how religious are you?", the consumer may say highly religious although he or she never attends religious services because he or she feels spiritually connected in the religion. Alternatively, if you ask a consumer "how often do you attend religious services?", the consumer may respond very frequently because he or she falls into the category of Sunday Christians just previously described. The person may frequently attend religious services, yet not actually practice the faith.

The seminal article addressing measurement of religiosity in consumer behavior proposes a four-factor model consisting of church attendance, importance of religious values, confidence in religious values, and self-perceived religiousness.[29] This article is one of the first and only attempts to create a standard for measuring religiosity across the field of consumer behavior. One concern with this model is that using church attendance makes the instrument not applicable to all world religions because some religions do not have regular church attendance (e.g., Confucianists and Taoists, who may attend classes during primary schooling but not weekly classes as adults).

Additionally, recent analysis of this four-factor model of religiosity reveals that dropping the church attendance component of the model does not significantly affect the predictive accuracy and, therefore, a three-component model without church attendance is sufficient.[30]

In another religiosity scale developed by Himmelfarb, behavioral (i.e., extrinsic) rather than internal (i.e., intrinsic) dimensions are the greatest descriptor of religiosity and account for the greatest amount of variance.[31] Therefore, highly religious individuals would be expected to behave differently, including during the consumption process. Himmelfarb identifies nine total dimensions to religiosity: devotional (observing rituals), doctrinal, experiential, affiliational (social aspect), ideological, intellectual-esthetic (e.g., religious study), affectional, ethical, and moral.[32]

Another model of religiosity includes six dimensions: belief, experience, religious practice, religious knowledge, individual moral consequences, and social consequences. This measure is reliable even after controlling for the effects of culture.[33] These dimensions are expanded from Faulkner and de Jong's original religiosity measurement scale that consisted of five dimensions: ideological, intellectual, ritualistic, experiential, and consequential.[34] In another widely used scale of religiosity by King and Hunt,[35] an initial multidimensional religiosity scale[36] was amended to include religious knowledge that was supported through replication.[37] However, Himmelfarb explicitly states that measuring religious knowledge is an inadequate measure of religiosity.[38] For example, a person could have memorized large portions of his or her religious scripture but not use that knowledge to guide everyday behavior, which then would be useless information for businesses to have.

Some measures of religiosity are very simple, only measuring church or synagogue attendance and financial contributions to the religious institution.[39] However, this religiosity measurement system fails to recognize the cognitive or internal aspects of religiosity. Hill and Hood's book, *Measures of Religiosity*, identifies 126 different academically supported scales/methods for measuring religiosity.[40] There is definitely a great variety in scales, so how is a business to know what scale to use? Popular use, reliability, and significant findings are several criteria that can be used to identify the appropriate religiosity scale to use. Researchers in consumer behavior and religion use Wilkes and colleagues' four-factor model of religiosity[41] and Allport and Ross' intrinsic and extrinsic models of religiosity most frequently.[42]

Allport and Ross'[43] Religious Orientation Scale dominates numerous studies.[44] Allport and Ross define four basic categories of religious orientation based upon one's intrinsic and extrinsic religious expression.[45] At the highly religious extreme is the person who is fully intrinsically and extrinsically religious, otherwise termed as "indiscriminately proreligious."[46] At the other extreme is the person who is neither intrinsically nor extrinsically religious, receiving the label of "indiscriminately antireligious or nonreligious."[47] Conservative religions are found more often to fall at the intrinsic end of the spectrum.[48] To show the importance of the use of intrinsic/extrinsic (I/E) orientation to measure religiosity, the *Journal for the Scientific Study of Religion* once committed a full issue just to the I/E topic.[49]

When looking for a universal religiosity measurement scale, it is important to realize that different religions use different measures to assess religiosity.[50] For example, Protestants tend to focus more on religious practice and belief but not as much on religious knowledge, whereas Jews tend to focus more on religious practice but not as much on religious belief or knowledge.[51] In addition, most religiosity scales were created for one culture, predominantly American Christians. Especially when conducting international religion research, new scales may be better suited to adapt to culture and affiliation differences.[52] For example, Muhamad and Mizerski used the adapted MARS (Muslim Attitudes toward Religion Scale), developed by Wilde and Joseph,[53] to more accurately assess Muslim religiosity.[54]

Muhamad and Mizerski developed a comprehensive model for measuring Muslim religiosity consisting of five predictors of consumer behavior: religious affiliation, religious commitment, religious knowledge, religious orientation, and consequences.[55] All of these predictors have been cited previously as important to an accurate measure of religiosity, but this study is the first attempt to group all aspects of religiosity into one comprehensive model.

The takeaway for businesses is that there are numerous different religiosity scales to use. The specific choice of scale should depend on its use and its measurement characteristics. If measuring across religious groups and cultures, Muhamad and Mizerski's comprehensive scale may be best.[56] If interested in devout versus "just for show" consumers, Allport and Ross' intrinsic/extrinsic scale may be better.[57] On the other hand, with ample time and a need for a more thorough picture of the religiosity of a target market, Himmelfarb's scale could provide a more comprehensive understanding of religiosity.[58] See Table 2.2 for a summary of religiosity scales and when they are best used.

Categories of Religious Affiliation

There is no all-encompassing standard for measuring differences between religions and their denominations/sects.[59] Allport and Ross separate Christian denominations into Catholic, Lutheran, Nazarene, Presbyterian, Methodist, and Baptist, although the standard in religious research is to separate Christian denominations into Catholic, Protestant, and Orthodox.[60] Protestant denominations can also be separated into Baptist, Reformed, Presbyterian, Methodist, Lutheran, and Disciples of Christ.[61] The most popular method for distinguishing between religious groups in the consumer behavior literature uses only Protestant, Catholic, and

Table 2.2. Religiosity Measurement Scales

Religiosity scale	Components	Creator	Best use
Multidimensional Spiritual Transcendence Scale	Personality factors & spirituality	Piedmont (1999)	Examining spirituality in relation to a consumer's other personality traits
Transcendence Index	Connection with God, maintenance of spiritual relationship, outcomes of spirituality	Seidlitz et al. (2002)	Assessing consumer spirituality
Consumer Behavior Religiosity Scale	Church attendance, importance of religious values, confidence in religious values, self-perceived religiousness	Wilkes, Burnett, & Howell (1986)	Consumer research among religious affiliations that attend church
Behavioral vs. Internal Religiosity Scale	Devotional, doctrinal, experiential, affiliational (social aspect), ideological, intellectual-esthetic (religious study), affectional, ethical, & moral	Himmelfarb (1975)	Comprehensive, detailed understanding of target market
Cross-cultural Religiosity Scale	Belief, experience, religious practice, religious knowledge, individual moral consequences, & social consequences	Dejong, Faulkner, & Warland (1976)	Cross-cultural research
Five-Dimension Scale of Religiosity	Ideological, intellectual, ritualistic, experiential, & consequential	Faulkner & Dejong (1966)	Understanding ideological beliefs and behaviors of unknown religious groups
Religious Variable Scale	Credal assent, devotionalism, congregational involvement, organizational activity, financial support, religious knowledge, orientation to religion, & religious salience	King & Hunt (1969)	Comprehensive assessment of religiosity for Christians
Consumer Religiosity Scale	Church/synagogue attendance & financial contributions to religious institution	McDaniel & Burnett (1990)	First step in understanding religiosity of customers
Religious Orientation Scale	Internal religiosity (e.g., prayer) & external religiosity (e.g., church attendance)	Allport & Ross (1967)	Examining devout vs. "just-for-show" levels of religiosity
Muslim Attitudes Toward Religion Scale (adapted)	Religious affiliation, religious commitment, religious knowledge, religious orientation, & consequences	Muhamad & Mizerski (2010)	Comparison among several religious affiliations

Note: These measures are the most used religiosity scales in the study of consumer behavior and may not represent the most used scales in other fields.

Jew,[62] and occasionally such studies include a "no religious affiliation" category.[63] One of the first consumer behavior studies divides Christian denominations into Lutheran or Assembly of God.[64]

Other research examines world religions, separating western religions into one category (Christianity and Islam), while grouping together eastern religions into another category (Hinduism, Buddhism, and Confucianism).[65] Essoo and Dibb differentiate between Hindus, Muslims, Catholics, and "Other" religious groups.[66] One of the most common religious group measurement systems for assessing all of the major world religions includes Protestant, Catholic, Buddhist, Hindu, Muslim, and Jew.[67] Particularly for companies operating in America, distinguishing between Protestants and Catholics, both types of Christians, is beneficial for understanding core beliefs, as will be described in the next chapter on belief systems of the western world. Clearly, there is a need for a standard in measuring religious affiliation that encompasses a larger set of religious affiliations to better define differences between religions and religious subgroups.

As many religions become fragmented and secularized with fundamentalists, reformists, and everyone in between, a measure of strict adherence to doctrine becomes increasingly important. One means for assessing doctrinal importance is to separate religions into conservative, orthodox, and secular religions.[68] Another similar measure of secularization is to separate religious affiliations into fundamentalists, liberals, or "ordinary" (meaning somewhere in the middle between fundamentalist and liberal), as was done with a study of religious Muslims.[69]

One of the more popular methods in the religious literature is to separate consumers within a religious affiliation by religious fundamentalism using Smith's classification system of Liberal, Moderate, or Conservative believers.[70] This classification system has been used to segment consumer behavior in a variety of fields, including religion and sociology.[71] In Hill and Hood's book of measurement instruments of religion, five fundamentalism scales are identified that should be considered by any researcher delving into religious research with the segmented religious groups of today.[72] These scales can help dissect adherence to specific beliefs (e.g., women's submission to men) that guide decision making and, for businesses, development of marketing campaigns.

One possible reason that researchers have failed to find more results attributable to religion is that religious categories have not been measured carefully enough. For example, the popular categorization of "Protestant, Catholic, or Jew" fails to recognize the wide variety within each category. Jewish consumers can be Orthodox, Conservative, or Reformed. Protestants include many denominations, some quite different from others. Even within a particular denominational label, great diversity can separate subgroups. For example, the two largest Lutheran groups are the LCMS [Lutheran Church–Missouri Synod] (example of a member, Rush Limbaugh) and the ELCA [Evangelical Lutheran Church in American] (example of a member at least in the past, Garrison Keillor). These two groups have quite different world views on a liberal versus conservative dimension, although they share much traditional Lutheran theology. Even their cultural histories differ, with the LCMS having more Germanic roots and the ELCA having more Scandinavian roots.

Because statistical tests of significance contrast variance within a group and variance between a group, if a categorization system is too broad, the two types of variance may not differ in spite of underlying diversity. The highly-visible Big Data movement in business research now allows the use of modern information-gathering and computing technology to parse information ever more precisely and to view religion through a new lens that allows us to see the relations among religions ever more clearly. Especially when theory tempers and directs these efforts, we can anticipate increasing benefits from understanding the role of religion in consumer decisions.

See Table 2.3 for a summary of religious classification systems. Although we describe what systems are "best used for," people should be cautious to use a system that is sufficiently complex for the purpose at hand. Too often investigators use overly-simplistic systems relative to their actual goals.

Interpreting Religious Data

When measuring religion, it is important to realize the potential for surveyor bias based upon the survey developer's religious beliefs, preconceived notions, and lack of knowledge of other religions. Having the

Table 2.3. Religious Classification Systems

Religious affiliations	Best used for
Catholic, Protestant, Orthodox	Research in Christian markets
Baptist, Reformed, Presbyterian, Methodist, Lutheran, Disciples of Christ	Detailed research within Protestant denominations
Protestant, Catholic, Jew, None	Identifying followers of the largest US religious groups
Christian, Muslim, Jew, Hindu, Buddhist, Taoist, Confucianist	Thorough research on all religious affiliations
Conservative, orthodox, secular	Determining the strict adherence to religious scripture
Liberal, moderate, conservative	Determining the strict adherence to religious scripture with a universally-known classification system

survey instrument reviewed by a knowledgeable adherent of each religion included in a study is one means for minimizing surveyor bias and improving accuracy of the findings.[73] In addition, gaining at least a baseline understanding of other religions' views will be crucial for understanding the religious beliefs of a company's target market and other niche markets. One of the major challenges in studying religion is that many of the consumers of the data and literature try to put their own spin on findings or try to distort results to reflect pre-conceived biases.

When interpreting the results of survey research, businesses should be aware that minority religions could be influenced by the beliefs of the majority religion.[74] Buddhists, in particular, are influenced by the majority religion when Buddhists are a minority religion.[75] Thus, religious groups may respond similarly to the majority group on a survey but could still hold different beliefs that guide certain daily decision making. To get at these unique differences, researchers can tailor questionnaires to specific religious beliefs and practices (e.g., calling a place of worship a church vs. synagogue vs. temple) and ensure unanimity with the survey results.

The process of actually collecting data relating to religion and associated characteristics can be challenging because of the taboo nature of religion. These challenges will be discussed in further detail in Chapter 5 with regard to the disconnect between belief systems and behavioral economics. For example, during intercept interviews, random consumers are intercepted in public places (e.g., mall, park) and asked to complete an interview. Respondents may feel inclined to answer according to the cultural trends of the area in order to fit in with the dominant group, rather than giving an accurate response. Touch cards can be used to allow a respondent to touch or click his or her answers to sensitive subject areas (e.g., religious affiliation, religiosity, internal/external religious commitment) in an effort to increase the accuracy of responses.[76]

To have a representative sample, a researcher would need to find a sample comprising of many different religious views; however, when talking about target markets, this representative sample would be indicative of who is currently and who is most likely to be purchasing a brand's products or services. Thus, the representative sample of users of one brand may be predominantly Protestant, Catholic, and atheist, while the representative sample of users for another brand may be predominantly Jewish, Muslim, and Buddhist.

The word *sample* here means that the entire target market is not being measured, rather a small section of the target market is measured. To predict the behaviors of a target market most accurately, this sample should have a demographic (e.g., age, religion, gender) profile that is representative of the entire target market. In other words, if the target market is 48% Protestant, 12% Muslim, 8% Hindu, and 2% Taoist with the rest atheists, then the sample should ideally also have this same composition. Additionally, if the target market is 70% female and 30% male, then the sample should also be representative of this full target market with 70% female and 30% male. Researchers have used a variety of methods to obtain representative samples including:

- Intercept interviews[77]
- Convenience samples through organizations/churches[78]
- Door-to-door samples (although these are decreasing with the increased ease of web surveys and the fear of con artists portraying door-to-door researchers)[79]
- Telephone random-digit dialing surveys[80]
- Survey samples based on product purchase records (e.g., store loyalty cards)[81]

- Mail out surveys (although these are decreasing with the increased reliance on the web)[82]
- Secondary data (i.e., data that have already been collected by others)[83]
- Web samples (e.g., email or social media surveys)[84]
- Student samples[85]

One of these sampling methods, when partnered with an accurate categorization method of religious affiliation and a religiosity measurement instrument, can then be used by businesses to better understand the brand's target market. Ideally, every consumer in the target market has an equal chance of being selected for the sample to be truly representative. Often researchers are satisfied if the proportions of consumers in the sample match the proportions of consumers in the target market population. See the Appendix for resources related to generalized estimates of religious presence in various geographic areas.

The next two chapters on Western and Eastern religions, respectively, will delve into how the identified religious makeup of a target market can be used to offer products and design marketing campaigns to address the target market's core values and belief systems. These chapters necessarily represent the systematic theology of religious groups, which does influence religious behavior of many but not all adherents, and at the same time places relatively less emphasis on individual spirituality.

CHAPTER 3

Belief Systems of the Western World & Interpretations for Behavioral Economics

Before delving into a discussion of specific religions, it is important to make the distinction between Western and Eastern religions. Seminal research in the field of religion and psychology posits distinct differences between Western religions (also known as the emissary religions) and Eastern religions (also known as the exemplary religions).[1] Western religions (Christianity, Judaism, Islam) are based on the same belief that God created the world and that there is a common truth (e.g., God created the world, end time with heaven/hell, etc.) that all must believe.[2] Eastern religions (Buddhism, Hinduism, Confucianism, Taoism), on the other hand, do not have a common truth but rather allow each adherent to seek individual truth through connection with a divine spirit, often through meditation.[3] In addition, Western religious doctrine states that God has control over nature, and the life achievement goal is heavenly life. In contrast, Eastern religious doctrine follows a pantheistic view that God is in and pervades all elements of nature, and the life achievement goal is enlightenment.[4]

This chapter explores the Western religions and how these religious beliefs influence consumer decision making. Chapter 4 examines the implications of Eastern religions on consumer decision making. However, we should note that because the focus is on religion's influence on behavioral economics, the description and history of each religion is limited, and thus not every belief of every religion is discussed and elaborated thoroughly. We recognize that this very brief review of the world's major religions only skims over thousands of years of world wisdom from dozens of disciplines, coming from very different angles. In fact, the challenge of summarizing religious beliefs is perhaps one of the reasons why so little research has been conducted on religion's influence on behavioral economics in the first place. We apologize in advance for any over-simplification that fails to capture the nuances of a particular belief system.

Christianity (Christians)

More than 2.2 billion people worldwide follow Christianity.[5] Christians fall into three main branches: Catholic, Protestant, and Orthodox.[6] Christians believe that God created the universe. God's son, Jesus, spread the news of God through testimony and miracles before dying and being resurrected from the dead.[7] Jesus died on the cross for all of humanity's sins and through faith in Jesus, people can be saved from eternal life in hell. Christian denominations differ on beliefs regarding exactly what is required for salvation. The purpose of the Christian life is to spread the word of God (i.e., evangelizing) and reach salvation. According to most denominations, salvation is reached through repenting of sins, asking forgiveness, and expressing faith in Jesus Christ. All Christians believe in the Trinity of Father God, Son Jesus Christ, and Holy Spirit representing the same being.[8]

Catholicism

Catholics and Protestants differ fundamentally as to whether or not a personal relationship with God is possible. Catholics believe that a relationship with God is guided through the priest. That is, God's grace is mediated through the sacraments, which are administered by priests. In contrast, Protestants believe that every individual can have a personal relationship with God without an intermediary, sometimes called the universal priesthood of all believers.[9] Catholics also define the Bible somewhat differently from most Protestants; they believe God's word can also be found in the seven apocryphal books and four semi-complete books, as well as traditions, councils, and the papacy.[10] Catholics often worship God in several services per week that are called Mass.[11]

Overview and Presence of the Catholic Belief System

Catholics represent the second largest religious affiliation in the United States with 25.1% of the U.S. religious adherents.[12] Another prominent national survey shows 23.9% of Americans are Catholic.[13] Of these Catholics, 29% are Latino, which is the largest proportion of Latinos in any religion in America.[14] More than 1.1 billion people worldwide are Catholic.[15]

Roman Catholics believe that the Catholic church is the way to salvation.[16] The Pope is the leader of all Catholics and guides the church bishops.[17] The Pope is believed to have inherited the apostle Peter's role from the Bible allowing the Pope's words to be supreme in all matters of faith and discipline.[18] Catholics believe in seven fundamental sacraments: baptism, confession of sin, communion, confirming faith in the Catholic church, marriage, holy orders for individuals to take on special roles in the church, and anointing the sick.[19]

How Catholicism Influences Behavioral Economics

The behavior of Catholic consumers is largely based upon direction from the Pope, who is believed to have direction from God. If the Pope makes a statement regarding participation in war, use of certain health procedures, or other statements related to acts of consumption, Catholic consumers are likely to follow. Thus, any company operating in Catholic predominant communities should stay abreast of communication between the Pope and followers of Catholicism.

Some Catholics today still do not believe in the use of birth control, although there has been a movement toward more acceptance of birth control among the faithful (though not in the official hierarchy). Several Catholic universities, such as Boston College and the University of Notre Dame, do not allow forms of birth control to be distributed on campus. Thus, businesses advertising birth control products should be cautious before advertising their products in areas of high Catholic presence. Also in relation to birth control, Catholics are strongly opposed to abortion. Any mention of abortion pills or abortion procedures should not be targeted toward Catholics or in Catholic predominant areas. Campaigns that discourage abortion and acknowledge the importance of the life of each individual (e.g., a March of Dimes campaign) would benefit from targeting Catholics and stating the company's anti-abortion views.

Because 29% of Catholics in the United States are Latino and many areas of the world have a strong Latino Catholic presence (e.g., South America), it is important for businesses to respect the interplay between Catholicism and the Latino heritage. Businesses selling ethnic products should consider targeting religious groups as religious core values define the core values of ethnic groups.

During the time of Lent (prayer and reflection period for the 40 days before Easter), Catholics do not eat meat on Friday. Companies desiring to target Catholics would benefit from offering non-meat meal ideas for Fridays. During the period of Lent, Catholics often give something up in remembrance of the time of Easter (i.e., when the savior Jesus died on the cross and rose again three days later). For example, a Catholic may give up fancy coffee drinks for 40 days and "sacrifice" by eating kale every day. Just as Jesus sacrificed His life, Catholics believe that sacrificing something in their lives is an act of remembrance for their salvation. Companies operating in heavily Catholic regions should be aware of the period of Lent and consider toning down advertising if selling a luxurious or otherwise hedonic product.

If desiring to use religious symbols in advertising, companies should be aware that Catholics place great emphasis on the Virgin Mary, the mother of the savior Jesus. Using the Virgin Mary in a positive, authentic light may gain Catholic acceptance; however, making a mockery of the Virgin Mary or other symbols of the Catholic faith (e.g., nuns) can cause Catholic consumers to quickly revolt against a brand and even fight for the advertisement to be banned.

Protestant

Protestants represent the most common religious affiliation in the United States with 49.8% of the population falling into this group.[20] Another survey shows that 51.3% of Americans are Protestant with 26.3% of adherents in evangelical churches, 18.1% in mainline churches, and 6.9% in historically black churches.[21] An extremely rough estimate projects that approximately 500 million people in the world are Protestant.[22]

All Protestants have three fundamental beliefs: the Bible is the authoritative word of God, salvation is by faith in Jesus Christ, and a personal relationship with God is possible for all without need for any intermediary.[23] This personal relationship with God without the need for an intermediary is what differentiates Catholics and Protestants (i.e., Catholics need a priest to be the intermediary). Within the Protestant belief system, there are numerous denominations that have slightly different views on religious practice (e.g., the role of women in the church, type of music to be played, acceptance of homosexuals), but all of these groups follow the three fundamental Protestant beliefs.[24] The largest of the Protestant denominations are reviewed below.

Overview and Presence of the Protestant Belief System

Baptist

Baptists represent 17.2% of Americans and 33.5% of American Protestants.[25] Worldwide, between 40 million[26] and 75 million people are Baptists.[27]

John Smyth founded the first Baptist church in 1611. The majority of Baptist churches allow only men in leadership positions in the church and reserve Baptism (a ritual performed after accepting Jesus as one's savior) and other religious sacraments only for the spiritually mature (i.e., no infant baptism).[28] Baptists today tend to be conservative believers (i.e., believing that the Bible is infallible and holding strongly to the commandments in the Bible), especially those belonging to churches in the Southern Baptist Convention.[29]

Methodist

Methodists represent 6.2% of Americans and 12.1% of American Protestants.[30] Worldwide, between 60 million[31] and 70 million people are Methodists.[32] John Wesley founded Methodism in the early 1700s.[33] Today, Methodists have church pastors who are governed by a general conference.[34]

Methodists are considered one of the more liberal Protestant denominations and focus on improving the quality of life for all humans rather than arguing over doctrinal differences.[35] Feeding the hungry, finding shelter for the homeless, and supporting the depressed are all encouraged in the Methodist Church. Methodists are very open to members regardless of race, gender, or sexual orientation and all can be ordained into the ministry.[36] Women represent 17% of ordained clergy worldwide in the United Methodist Church.[37]

Lutheran

Lutherans represent 4.6% of Americans and 9.0% of American Protestants.[38] Worldwide, between 65 million[39] and 75 million people are Lutheran.[40] Martin Luther, often considered the founder of Protestantism, headed the Lutheran movement in the 1500s while protesting against the practices and teaching of the Catholic church.[41]

The Lutheran doctrine is detailed in the Book of Concord and is followed by most Lutherans today.[42] Lutherans believe the Bible is the inspired word of God.[43] Churches are autonomous, allowing each church to select pastors, manage property, and so forth.[44] Also, some Lutherans do not allow women to be ordained into the ministry (except for some churches such as the Evangelical Lutheran Church of America), follow law and gospel closely, and have generally conservative views.[45]

Non-denominational

Non-denominational adherents represent 4.5% of Americans and 8.9% of American Protestants.[46] Religious views can run from extremely conservative to extremely liberal depending on the specific church. Many non-denominational churches are formed in an effort to unite Christians who are fragmented because of minor doctrinal differences (e.g., views about music, roles of women in the church).

Pentecostal

Pentecostals represent 4.4% of Americans and 8.5% of American Protestants.[47] Worldwide, between 130 million[48] and 150 million people are Pentecostals.[49] Agnes Ozman is known as the founder of the Pentecostal church in 1901.[50]

The fundamental distinction between Pentecostals and other Christian denominations is their belief in the gift of speaking in tongues.[51] Pentecostals believe that humans are filled with the Holy Spirit (a gift from God for those who have accepted Jesus as their savior) when they are able to speak in tongues. Speaking in tongues stems from the 50-day festival of Pentecost that concluded with the apostles speaking in tongues.[52] Women are allowed to fill any leadership positions in the church.[53] Most Pentecostals also believe in baptism by immersion only and some require foot washing prior to Holy Communion.[54]

Presbyterian

Presbyterians represent 2.7% of Americans and 5.2% of American Protestants.[55] Worldwide, approximately 80 million people are Presbyterians.[56] John Calvin and John Knox founded the Presbyterian church in the early 1500s[57] as part of the church reform movement.[58]

The role of women in the church varies depending on the level of conservativism of each church. The two largest Presbyterian churches (Presbyterian Church in America and Presbyterian Church USA) hold more liberal views of gender roles and allow women to be ordained as elders and ministers.[59] Presbyterians believe that Jesus Christ is spirituality present in the Holy Communion sacramental elements (i.e., bread representing the body of Christ and juice/wine representing the blood of Christ).[60] In addition, Presbyterians believe that once they are "saved" by God, they can never lose this salvation.[61]

Restorationist

Restorationists, known just as Christian churches by some,[62] include the Church of Christ and Disciples of Christ and represent 2.1% of Americans and 4.0% of American Protestants.[63] Worldwide, four million people are Restorationists.[64]

The goal of Restorationists is to bring unity back to the Christian people who have become so fragmented because of minor doctrinal differences.[65] Some Restorationists, such as conservative Disciples of Christ, do not support instrumental music during services.[66] Other Restorationists strictly oppose abortion, the death penalty, and any other activities that can be viewed as war related.[67] Views regarding the second coming of the Lord, heaven, and hell are open to each individual's interpretation.[68]

Anglican/Episcopal

Anglicans and Episcopalians represent 1.5% of Americans and 3.0% of American Protestants.[69] Worldwide, 77 million people are Anglican or Episcopal.[70] The Episcopal and Anglican churches stem from the church of England that broke off from the Roman Catholic church in the early 1500s.[71]

Bishops are the heads of the church, and the pope is not supported.[72] Episcopal churches in particular follow several communal worship ceremonies (e.g., the Book of Common Prayer), doctrinal beliefs (e.g., the Thirty-Nine Articles of Religion), and written creeds (e.g., Apostle's creed, Nicene Creed) that assist in creating a communal body of the church.[73] Episcopalians, in particular, believe that baptism is required for salvation in addition to the Holy Communion.[74]

Holiness

Holiness followers include believers in the Church of the Nazarene and the Free Methodist Church, representing 1.2% of Americans and 2.2% of American Protestants.[75] The Holiness church broke off from the Methodist church in the late 1800s.[76] The Holiness church desired to retain its belief that perfectionism from sin was possible.[77]

Many behaviors are dictated by the Holiness churches through prohibition of smoking, drinking, visiting cinemas, dancing, listening to certain types of music, or wearing flashy clothes or makeup.[78] While most Holiness churches do not support women in any role in the ministry, some Nazarene churches (classified under Holiness churches) do allow women to be ordained into the ministry.[79] Baptism by immersion is essential for all, and foot washing prior to partaking in the Holy Communion is required by some Holiness churches.[80] Most Holiness churches are among the very few Christian churches that believe in speaking in tongues.[81]

Congregationalist

Congregationalists are affiliated with the United Church of Christ and represent 0.8% of Americans and 1.5% of American Protestants.[82] John Robinson, one of the initial leaders of the church, helped spread Congregationalism in America in the 1620s.[83]

The foundation of Congregationalist views is the belief that every congregation should have complete authority rather than having a general conference to report to.[84] Congregationalists are in stark contrast to the Episcopalians who fully support the church hierarchy.[85] Social activism, peace (no war related activities), openness to all races and sexes, and conservatism are very important to Congregationalists.[86] At the same time, each church is permitted to make rulings on the role of women in the church.[87]

Adventist

Adventists, primarily composed of the Seventh-Day Adventists, represent 0.5% of Americans and 0.9% of American Protestants.[88]

Originally founded by William Miller in 1816, Adventists believe in an imminent physical and visible second coming of Christ.[89] Seventh day Adventists in particular observe Saturday as a day of rest and free of work to prepare for the Lord's imminent arrival.[90] Adventists believe in several sacraments (elements of external religiosity) such as Baptism by immersion and foot washing in preparation for the Lord's Supper.[91] Some Adventists believe members should not participate in war.[92] Many Adventists also follow the dietary restrictions described in the Old Testament of the Bible.[93] For example, Adventists are prohibited from consuming alcohol and are advised to avoid caffeine.

Protestant Alternative Traditions and Off-Shoots

Followers of the alternative Protestant traditions and off-shoots do not believe that God, Jesus Christ, and the Holy Spirit (i.e., the trinity) are all the same being. Instead, followers of these alternative traditions and off-shoots believe that Jesus is a son a God, which is a distinctly different being from God. These followers also do not believe in certain portions of the 66 books of the Protestant Bible.[94]

LDS (Mormons)

Mormons comprise 1.7% of Americans.[95] Along with Muslims, Mormons have the largest family sizes in America.[96] Joseph Smith founded the Mormon religion in 1822 after receiving divine guidance about where gold tablets inscribed with the word of God were buried.[97] These tablets became the basis of the Book of Mormon, also known as Another Testament of Jesus Christ, which now represents the foundation of Mormon beliefs.[98] Mormons are adherents to the Church of Jesus Christ of Latter-Day Saints (LDS).

Mormons do not believe in the Trinity but instead believe that Jesus is a son of God. Believers should pattern their lives and actions after Jesus' and God's actions. Every individual can reach a level equal to that of Jesus. Another distinctive element of the Mormon religion is the belief in modern-day revelation and prophets (i.e., people today can be called by God to share God's insights with the earthly world). Mormons are well known for door-to-door proselytizing by missionaries, often by young men as a rite of passage and as a way to share the Mormon faith with nonbelievers.

Central to the Mormon's beliefs is the restoration of the true church.[99] Mormons adhere to many prohibitions issued by the LDS church including prohibitions against alcohol, stimulants, and caffeine. Also, Mormons honor the Sabbath day (Sunday) by worshipping God and not working outside the home on this day.

Additionally, endowed members of the church are required to tithe 10% of their income to the church and follow certain regulations before entering LDS temples (e.g., wearing temple-appropriate garments). Only endowed members of the LDS church are allowed to enter LDS temples. In addition, traditional gender roles are encouraged with females staying at home to care for the children and men exercising leadership roles and bringing in the family's income. These gender roles come from the belief that God has given women and men distinctly different roles in life.

Jehovah's Witness

Jehovah's Witness comprise just 0.7% of Americans.[100] Charles Taze Russell founded Jehovah's Witnesses in the late 1800s.[101]

The beliefs of Jehovah's Witnesses center around the imminent arrival of God's kingdom. Jehovah's Witnesses do not believe in the Trinity but rather believe that Jesus is only a son of God. Jehovah's Witnesses are well known to be door-to-door proselytizers, similar to the Mormons, in an attempt to sell *The Watchtower* (an interpretation of the end of the world and world events).[102] In contrast to Christians, Jehovah's Witnesses believe that Jesus died on a stake, not on a cross.[103]

Followers of Jehovah's Witness participate (and do not participate) in many activities that can have a great effect on consumer behavior. For example, followers are told that celebrating holidays and birthdays is immoral, blood transfusions are prohibited, and saluting any flag or participating in military service is forbidden.[104] Thus, any advertising encouraging holiday celebration would be offensive to strong adherents to the Jehovah's Witness faith. *The Watchtower* creed lists numerous other prohibitions and required actions for Jehovah's Witness followers.

How Protestantism Influences Behavioral Economics

Some conservative Protestants are encouraged to practice behaviors that are in strict accordance with the ten commandments of the biblical book of Exodus, including not lusting toward others. These behaviors would include dressing more conservatively (e.g., no excessively revealing clothing). Non-lustful behaviors also include a strict prohibition against pornography and any sexually explicit or provocative material on websites, in movies, in magazines, or elsewhere. Thus, companies involved in lust-filled industries should be cautious in marketing in areas that are predominantly conservative Protestant.

Some Protestant denominations also discourage or fully prohibit alcohol and caffeine. It is important for companies to not only understand the broad religious group that consumers follow (e.g., Christian, Jew, Muslim) but also the specific denomination (e.g., Baptist, Seventh Day Adventist) to better understand beliefs and restrictions that the consumer group follows.

Although there are no requirements that Protestants should attend Christian K-12 or college schooling, many Protestants choose to do so. Other schools that desire to recruit more Protestants could benefit from acknowledging acceptance of people from all beliefs and also emphasize their commitment to common moral values (e.g., single sex dorms to prevent sex before marriage, strong rules against cheating on tests, opportunities to get involved with church groups near campus). Providing Protestants a way to keep their religious identity (i.e., keep connected with religious groups) can make both the student and parents more likely to consider options other than Christian schooling.

All Protestants are encouraged to donate a portion of their earnings back to the church. Some Protestant denominations recommend that a "tithe" (10% of the income) is to be donated. This concept is important for all businesses to understand as the tithe decreases the level of discretionary income each consumer has. Non-profit organizations that follow the values of conservative Protestant denominations (e.g., no sex before marriage, no abortion, help the needy) could increase donations by specifically targeting Protestants in advertising. Most Protestants are encouraged to donate beyond the expected church donation to other organizations with Christian values.

Any companies in the music or entertainment industries should realize the competition from Christian music artists and Christian programming. In most Protestant churches, popular Christian songs are played, and members of the church are encouraged to listen to Christian music at home. Non-Christian artists should acknowledge the importance of Christian music to a Protestant while offering the non-Christian music as an alternative when desiring a change in music (e.g., upbeat music for workouts).

Although promoting Protestant values can be beneficial for a Protestant target market, companies should be cautious to avoid offending non-believers. For example, when non-believing consumers became aware that the fast food chain, Chick-fil-A, was supporting anti-gay Christian organizations, many non-believers boycotted Chick-fil-A. At the same time, strong Protestant believers increased their frequency and presence at Chick-fil-A locations. It is important to note that Chick-fil-A never openly stated that it is a Christian organization, but small actions can speak strongly about a company's values. Thus, there is an important balance and decision that businesses must make in understanding the religious affiliation of their consumer base, communicating a commit-ment to supporting these religious values, yet also being cautious not to offend consumers holding to other religious or no religious views.

Orthodox

One of the fundamental differences between Orthodox followers and other Christian followers is that the Orthodox believe that Jesus Christ is spiritually present in the sanctified elements of Holy Communion (i.e., bread representing Christ's body and grape juice/wine representing Christ's blood).[105] Additionally, Orthodox followers believe strongly in following tradition, which includes using ancient creeds and rituals.[106] The role of the Bible in the church is significantly less than in other Christian denominations with the Orthodox believing the meaning of the Bible should be interpreted by each church.[107] Thus, the importance of theology is less in the Orthodox church.

Overview and Presence of the Orthodox Belief System

Orthodox represent the smallest of the three main Christian seg-ments (Catholic, Protestant, Orthodox) in America with just 0.6% of Americans, who are separated into Greek Orthodox (less than 0.3%) and Russian Orthodox (less than 0.3%).[108] This means that there are just over one million Orthodox believers in the United States. However, world-wide Orthodox followers represent a significantly greater proportion of religious believers with over 200 million followers around the world.[109] The greatest proportion of these live in Russia (39% of Orthodox believ-ers worldwide) and at a distant second Ethiopia (13.9% of Orthodox believers) and Ukraine (13.4% of Orthodox believers); in total 76.9% of Orthodox believers reside in Europe with only 1.0% in the Americas.[110]

Marriage of ordained ministers is not allowed but is allowed prior to ordainment.[111] Orthodox followers believe that the Orthodox church is the only true church and the means to salvation.[112] The Russian Ortho-dox church still has a strong number of followers today, particularly in the Aleutian Islands in southwest Alaska, where the church first spread into America.[113]

How Orthodox Beliefs Influence Behavioral Economics

Because tradition is very important, Orthodox believers are more likely to buy religious items that support these traditions (e.g., copies of famous creeds or prayers, books related to God being present in elements of the Holy Communion). Social media outlets will also influence the purchase behavior of Orthodox believers, specifically those outlets that incorporate religious tradition (e.g., phone apps that allow for partaking in rituals or creeds while on the go, Facebook groups that provide suggestions of companies that support the Orthodox mission).

Tradition is also important during times of marriage and funerals for Orthodox believers and thus these believers would be more likely to look for wedding planners and funeral directors that accept these traditions—conducting ceremonies in the church, understanding the importance of prayer during these events, and being respectful of other church traditions before integrating event planning skills from the non-church world.

Orthodox believers also place great importance on holy icons, especially within the church.[114] This suggests that holy icons outside the church would also be valued, such as holy murals to hang up in the home, small replicas of statues of religious figures (e.g., a statue of Mary, Jesus' mother), or be interested in hiring artists who could paint murals in one's home.

Islam (Muslims)

Muslims are followers of the monotheistic Islamic religion dating back to the 7th century AD.[115] Muslims believe in one God (Allah) and God's prophet Muhammad. Muhammad received divine inspiration from God, which is what the Islamic religious book, the Qur'an, is based upon.[116] Interestingly, Muslims also believe that Jesus from the Christian religion is a prophet of God, just not the prophet who received divine inspiration from God. The Islamic religion is built on five pillars: *shahada* (professing one's faith), *salat* (prayer five times per day), *saum* (fasting during the month of Ramadan), *zakat* (charity tax to poor), and *hajj* (pilgrimage to Mecca).[117]

Overview and Presence of the Muslim Belief System

In America, only 0.6% of the population is Muslim, which can be organized into Sunni (0.3%), Shi'a (less than 0.3%), and others (less than

0.3%).[118] Along with Mormons, Muslims have the largest family sizes in America with 15% of Muslim adults having three or more children at home.[119] Around the world, there are approximately one billion[120] to 1.2 billion Muslims with inhabitants in almost every country.[121] Most Muslims live in Asia (550 million), the Middle East (306 million), and Africa (150 million).[122]

The two main sects in Islam are Sunni (most of the world's Muslims) and Shi'ite.[123] Shi'ite followers, called Shi'a Muslims, live primarily in Iran and Iraq whereas Sunni Muslims represent between 85% and 90% of the world's Muslims.[124] The foundational difference between Sunni and Shi'a Muslims is the belief in what happened after the prophet Muhammad died. Sunni Muslims believe that no person can take the divine role that Muhammad had and that leaders could only interpret Muhammad's writings.[125] Shi'a Muslims, on the other hand, believe that Muhammad's ancestors could take over the divine guidance role that Muhammad previously had.[126]

How Islam Influences Behavioral Economics

Islam is much more than just a religion; it is a way of life.[127] One of the predominant forces driving Muslim consumer behavior is products or activities that are *halal*, an Arabic word meaning allowed.[128] At the other extreme are *haram* items or activities that are prohibited or highly discouraged. Islamic scholars (the *Ulama*) study *Shariah* law and issue *fatwas* to prohibit the use of certain products, services, or related behaviors when they would be detrimental to religious beliefs.[129]

For example, *halal* cosmetics do not contain alcohol or the fat of swine, and use of *halal* financial services is required to guarantee no person takes financial advantage of another person.[130] *Haram* products include alcohol, liquor, wine, non-Shariah gelatin (depends on the source of the gelatin), and cheese made from swine.[131] Muslims are also forbidden from consuming pork,[132] gambling, cheating, worshipping idols, adultery, and indecent exposure.[133] When Muslims do consume meat, the meat must be *halal*, which requires that the meat is slaughtered by a Muslim, God's name (*Allah*) is used during the time of slaughter, and the animal throat is sliced with a sharp blade.

Even if products are not explicitly *haram* (e.g., cereal, pasta, salad), these products could be composed of ingredients that are *haram* (e.g., animal shortening, gelatin, alcohol, cheese from animal enzymes), therefore making the product not allowed to be consumed.[134] For example, while Hershey's Chocolate Milk Mix is allowed, Hershey's Chocolate Marshmallow Drink is not because one ingredient of marshmallows is often gelatin—a *haram* product. Similarly, Quaker's Marshmallow Flavored Crisp Rice Cereal is *haram*. Additionally, many salad dressings and sauces include small amounts of wine, such as Heinz's Dijon Mustard, which includes small amounts of white wine and is therefore a *haram* product.

Haram products do not apply just to food products but also to other products that come in contact with the body, such as lotions and toothpaste. For example, several varieties of Mentadent and Sensodyne toothpaste contain gelatin, and numerous brands of mouthwash use alcohol as a primary ingredient for killing bacteria in the mouth making both of these products *haram*. Any business with Muslim consumers, especially international businesses distributing products in Muslim-predominant countries, must become intimately aware of *haram* items and issued *fatwas* to be successful.

In addition, conservative Muslim women are required to wear a *burqa* (a full body covering) and a *hijab* (hair covering) as a gesture of modesty. This means that clothing worn underneath the burqa will not be seen by the general public. Thus, ads featuring women in elaborate clothing would not be a means of identity expression as it would be for non-Muslim women. Views of the necessity to wear a facial covering differ by culture and sect. Many Muslim women who wear the full burqa seek out other means of wealth and identity expression. For example, Muslim women in the more wealthy, oil-supported Arab countries are found wearing gold jewelry on the outside of the burqa. Muslim women may also spend more money on cosmetics because these can be worn around the eyes, one of the few spots visible on the body when the burqa is worn. However, international companies should be cautious targeting women because of advertising restrictions set by national governments and ad councils.

Judaism (Jews)

Jews, similar to Christians, believe that one God created the world and follow the ten commandments, inclusive of 613 commandments in all.[135]

Jews believe in the first half of the Christian bible (the old testament) and hold the first five books of the old testament (the *torah*) most sacred. Jews also believe that a savior to free the world from sin has yet to come. Thus, Jews do not believe that Jesus from the Christian religion is the son of God. Three fundamental beliefs are supported by Jews: *torah* (religious study), *avodah* (worship), and *gemilut chasadim* (giving back/ repairing the world).[136] In general, Jews are focused more on religious practice than on religious belief or knowledge.[137] This distinction between religious practice and belief stems from the difference between secular Judaism (i.e., following history and values but not the Torah) and religious Judaism (i.e., acceptance of the Torah).[138]

Overview and Presence of the Jewish Belief System

Jews represent 1.7% of Americans, which can be broken down into reformed (0.7%), conservative (0.5%), orthodox (less than 0.3%), or other (0.3%).[139] Worldwide, more than 16 million people are Jewish.[140] The vast majority of Jews today live in the United States and Israel.[141] Jews and Christians stem from the same Abrahamic roots, dating back to at least 2000 BC.[142] Judaism is the oldest monotheistic religion in the world that is still practiced today.[143]

Divisions within Judaism stem from focus on fundamental beliefs with these divisions separating Jews into conservative Jews (33% worldwide), reformed Jews (22%), orthodox Jews (17%), and unaffiliated Jews (28%).[144] Orthodox Jews are the most conservative in contrast to Conservative Jews who adapt Jewish beliefs to modern culture. Conservative Jews are the most populous Jewish sect in America. Reformed Jews are the most liberal of the Jewish sects. Finally, unaffiliated Jews can carry a variety of fundamentalism views.[145]

How Judaism Influences Behavioral Economics

Businesses desiring to target Jews need to be especially cautious given the over 600 laws Jews are instructed to follow. Encouraging behaviors that are not in accordance with these laws would likely lose Jewish following and possibly even create anti-brand sentiment, especially for Orthodox

Jews. For example, male Jews are required to wear a small leather case with scriptures on the arm after age 13.[146] Clothing companies desiring to target Jews should be cautious in creating advertisements that would inhibit the ability to wear these scriptures. However, some conservative Jews and most reformed Jews do not follow each of these 600 laws. Thus, it is essential for businesses to understand where a target market resides in terms of fundamentalism within Judaism.

Under strict observation of Jewish law, marriage is restricted to only other Jews.[147] The Jewish marriage ceremony is unique in its customs, and thus companies in the wedding business desiring to target Jews should be aware of the unique wedding regalia and customs involved. Jews also hold specific views on how to mourn and pray, which can be important for any business involved in end-of-life practices (e.g., mortuaries, cemeteries, life insurance).[148]

Jews follow many food restrictions that are critical to understand for any business involved in the food industry. Kosher dietary restrictions influence many Jews.[149] Although many laws are not followed strictly, most practicing Jews follow some Kosher requirements. Interestingly, many agnostic and atheist consumers are now coming to prefer Kosher foods because of the perception that Kosher foods are healthier and more natural than other foods.[150]

Jews consider non-permissible foods to be *halakhah*, which are iden-tified both in the Torah (the first five books of the Bible) and through guidance from religious leaders (also known as rabbis).[151] *Halakhah* foods include animal meat from animals that do not chew their cud and are not slaughtered in a ritual manner.[152] Jews are also not permitted to consume pork.[153] Additionally, Jews cannot consume meat and dairy at the same meal. In other words, companies should not engage in bundle advertising featuring meat and dairy products together. For Jews, even utensils, pots, and pans for meat and dairy products should be kept separate. Thus, ads featuring cheese and meat being cooked in the same pot or meals of meat and cheese (e.g., a cheeseburger) should not be targeted at Jewish consumers.

In terms of activities, Sundays are a day of rest for Jewish consum-ers. Stores should not promote sales on Sundays. In addition, employ-ers desiring to hire Jewish employees should not expect Jews to work on Sundays. Rather, Jews believe that Sundays should be day of rest and reflection on God.

Businesses are beginning to realize the benefit of targeting the Jewish market. For example, a new site called Jdeal, the Jewish version of Groupon, was developed to focus on Kosher deals and entertainment packages.[154] Although the Jewish market is smaller than some other religious markets, there are still 16 million Jewish consumers around the world making it important for businesses to understand Jewish culture and consider Jews as a niche target market.

CHAPTER 4

Belief Systems of the Eastern World & Interpretations for Behavioral Economics

Several religious belief systems have roots more in Asia than in Europe and the Middle East. Although these religions are not as prominent in North America, their presence nevertheless exerts an influence on at least some consumers in the United States. This chapter considers the largest of these Eastern religions.

Buddhism (Buddhists)

Buddhists follow the teachings of Buddha written in the Tripitaka and Sutras.[1] Buddhists do not worship any Gods; instead, Buddhists seek mental departure from the material world.[2] The goal in the life of a Buddhist is to reach enlightenment.[3] Buddha emphasized human transformation into selfless beings helping others rather than oneself, a process described as *bodhisattva*.[4] Four noble truths represent the foundation of Buddhist beliefs: *dukkha* (suffering or stress, a defining aspect of life), *dukkha* is caused by *tanha* (clinging to material, tangible items), *dukkha* can end with *nirvana* (reaching heaven state free of suffering), and an end to *dukkha* can be reached by following the Eightfold Path to ultimate enlightenment and a new state of reality.[5]

Overview and Presence of the Buddhist Belief System

In America, only 0.7% of the population is Buddhist, which can be broken down into Zen Buddhist (less than 0.3%), Theravada Buddhist (0.3%), Tibetan Buddhist (less than 0.3%), and other (0.3%).[6]

Buddhism began in India in the sixth and fifth centuries BCE with the enlightened one, Siddhartha Gautama (otherwise known as Buddha).[7] Over 350 million people worldwide follow Buddhism, most of whom are found in East Asia.[8]

The two main divisions in Buddhism are Theravada Buddhism (following the teachings of Buddha and elders) and Mahayana Buddhism (focusing on meditation and monastic life).[9] Theravada Buddhist's believe that the path to enlightenment is in the individual's hands and that no God or other supernatural being exists. In contrast, Mahayana Buddhists believe that the path to enlightenment is influenced by other aspects of life (not just the individual's) and also that there is a supernatural power that can extend grace. While the Theravada Buddhist's goal is to seek wisdom, the Mahayana Buddhist's goal is to seek and spread compassion.[10]

Although many outsiders think of Buddhist temples as the representation of all Buddhism, these temples are most critical to Theravada Buddhists, who believe that spiritual development must take place inside temples. Mahayana Buddhists, on the other hand, believe that spiritual development can occur anywhere—including inside one's home.[11] While Theravada Buddhists are primarily found in southeast Asia (Thailand, Burma, Sri Lanka, Laos), Mahayana Buddhists are found more in northeast Asia (China, South Korea, Japan, Vietnam).[12]

Other Buddhism divisions are Vajrayana/Tantric Buddhism, Pure Land Buddhism, Tibetan Buddhism, and Zen Buddhism, which are further divisions of the beliefs of Theravada and Mahayana Buddhism.[13]

How Buddhism Influences Behavioral Economics

Much of Buddhism's influence on consumer behavior can be summed up by the Buddhist Eightfold Path, *samma*. This path consists of right thought/attitude, intention, speech, conduct/action, livelihood/occupation, effort, awareness, and concentration.[14] Along this path, Buddhists follow 10 precepts of actions that are prohibited and that businesses should be well aware of: killing, stealing, indulging in sexual pleasure, lying, becoming intoxicated, eating after noon, dancing/singing/playing instruments, using perfumes or makeup, using excessive seats/beds, and handling gold/silver.[15] Each of these precepts can have numerous implications for consumer behavior. For example, companies involved in the production of makeup or instruments should not target Buddhists who live by the Eightfold Path. In addition, jewelry makers desiring to target Buddhists should avoid the use of gold and silver. Furniture makers desiring to target Buddhists should emphasize simple and not luxurious furniture models.

As with any religion, believers of Buddhism have varying beliefs regarding their principle commandments. Although some Buddhists feel that the "killing is prohibited" precept of action refers only to other humans, other Buddhists believe that this precept applies to all animals and are therefore strict vegetarians.[16] Thus, if a company is selling meat products in a Buddhist area, market research should first determine the Buddhists' general views on killing as a precept to action. If killing refers to all animals, businesses selling vegetarian products would benefit from emphasizing the importance of all life and developing a niche target market toward Buddhists.

Along the eightfold path, Buddhists see the importance of "right speech" as a reflection of internal character. This view has implications for marketing communications as well as design of new product offerings. For example, a violent movie whose heroic character frequently uses vulgar language would be offensive to Buddhists. In addition, any spokespeople or celebrity endorsers used by brands should exhibit morally proper speech and conduct if Buddhists are to be targeted.

Just as Buddhism influences consumption, Buddhism also influences anti-consumption. One of the four noble truths of Buddhism, *dukkha,* derived from materialism, addresses the desire for material goods that Buddhists are supposed to avoid. Many Buddhists believe, "When we are selfless, we are free."[17] Thus, advertisements depicting consumers giving into their desires would be against one of the four noble truths of the Buddhist religion. Companies should emphasize the purpose of goods and services rather than how these objects fulfill potentially dubious desires. In addition, goods and services that are primarily created to fulfill desires (e.g., beauty products, expensive electronic products, and products emphasizing personal sexual satisfaction) should be cautiously targeted when dealing with Buddhist consumers.

Hinduism (Hindus)

Hinduism has its roots in India, where approximately 80% of India's inhabitants are Hindus.[18] The religious texts of Hinduism are the *Vedas* consisting of *Samhitas, Brahmamas, Upanishads,* and *Sutras.*[19] Worship is an important aspect of Hinduism with most Hindus.[20] A search for simplicity and purification in life forms the foundation of Hinduism.[21] So many different beliefs and scriptures make it very difficult to succinctly list the specific beliefs of Hindus.[22] Many followers worship through yoga.[23]

Overview and Presence of the Hindu Belief System

In America, only 0.4% of the population is Hindu.[24] Well over one billion people worldwide consider themselves Hindu, with the majority of followers in India.[25] The God, Brahma, created Hinduism. This God is no longer worshipped today because Brahma's sole role to create the universe is over.[26] Despite this God being no longer worshipped, Hindus believe in and worship numerous other Gods and, therefore, Hinduism is considered a polytheistic religion.[27]

Hinduism is considered one of the oldest world religions that is still followed today.[28] There are four main sects in Hinduism: *Shaivism* (worshipping Shiva as God), *Shaktism* (worshipping Shakti as the Divine Mother), *Vaishnavism* (worshipping Vishnu or other avatars), and *Smartism* (worshipping all Gods; liberal).[29] Each division has different views on the authority of religious scriptures, but most denominations hold strongly to the *Vedas* and *Agamas.*

Hindus believe in a cycle of rebirth where one's soul reincarnates continuously until all harmful actions are resolved and a personal connection with God is made. Many Hindus still follow a caste system where people are born into a place in society where they stay and are meant to be (e.g., some people are meant to be leaders whereas others are meant to be followers). Hindus supporting the caste system follow four main castes: (1) *Brahmins,* who are intellectual and spiritual leaders, (2) *Kshatriyas,* who are leaders and administrators, (3) *Vaishyas,* who are trade workers, such as farmers, and (4) *Shudras,* who are followers and often unskilled labor.[30]

In addition, Hindus follow three main pillars of practice: temple worship, scripture, and religious traditions. These religious traditions include such actions as meditative yoga, reciting portions of the scriptures, and pilgrimage.[31] Hindus follow four basic goals in life: *karma* (physical and emotional pleasure), *artha* (status achievement through fame, money, and power), *dharma* (following moral values), and *moksha* (ceasing the endless cycle of life and death).[32] Also, Hindus believe in *ahimsa* (i.e., non-violence), sacredness of cows, and, for some, vegetarianism.[33]

How Hinduism Influences Behavioral Economics

Businesses targeting Hindus should not market products including beef, which would offend the Hindu's belief about the sacredness of cows. For example, in 2002 McDonald's came under fire for labeling french fries and hash browns as vegetarian when in fact they were found to be fried in oil with trace amounts of beef. Hindu followers were outraged after learning that they had unknowingly consumed beef. As a result, McDonald's donated $10 million to Hindu and other related groups.[34] In India today, McDonald's offers Hindu-friendly menu items.

Along these lines, any business targeting Hindus or operating in a community that is predominantly Hindu would benefit from declaring the presence of beef in a product. Even if a product contains beef, alerting the consumer to this may lead a Hindu consumer to feel more favorably toward the brand because they are acknowledging Hindu beliefs. Although Hindus would not consume the beef product, they may be more apt to consume other products by the brand and share the positive news of brand efforts via word of mouth to friends and family.

Because many Hindus use yoga as a means for meditating and connecting with the Hindu Gods, companies offering yoga could target Hindus. However, yoga companies should be cautious in marketing campaigns to still be respectful of Hindu beliefs as well as the sincerity and sacredness of the yoga experience. Other products and services that enhance concentration and the meditating experience (e.g., music, candles, calming therapy) could also benefit from targeting Hindus.

When desiring to target Hindus, companies should know that Hindus often try to live near temples because of the importance of temple worship.[35] Thus, a company could search Hindu temples in a country and target offerings that may interest Hindus in those locations.

Confucianism/Taoism

Confucianism represents the teachings of Confucius, which is a dominant religion or philosophy (depending on how religion is defined) in China, Japan, Korea, and other places in East Asia.[36] Confucianism began in China in the 5th century BC[37] from the teachings of K'ung Fu-tzu.[38] The Confucian Classics, or *Analects*, are the sacred texts followed by Confucianists.[39] Confucianism is generally considered a religion as well as a philosophy because of the answers to life's purpose and the guidance for everyday behavior.[40] Confucian teachings focus on humanism and transcendence and, more specifically, seek to follow the basic moral rule to treat others in the same way that one wants to be treated.[41]

Taoism, also known as Daoism, is another philosophically based Chinese religion. Philosophical followers are termed tao-chia or *daojia* whereas religious followers are termed tao-chiao or *daojiao*.[42] Taoism teachings focus on internal transformation that results in morally good societies and behavior.[43] Tao, meaning "the way," reflects a lack of struggle and taking life as it comes.[44] Taoists believe that immortality can be achieved through control of the body with breathing exercises called *ch'i*.[45] In addition, some Taoists believe in the spirits of the *yin* and the *yang*.[46] Religion, theology, and philosophy are intertwined in this system.

Overview and Presence of the Confucian/Taoist Belief System

Over 6 million people worldwide are Confucian.[47] Confucians are mostly found in North Korea (traditionally Confucian, although suppressed) and Malaysia (less than 3% of population are Confucian or Taoist). Taoists, on the other hand, are mostly found in China (although less than 3% of the population), Malaysia (less than 3%), Singapore (around 8% of the population), and Taiwan (93% of population a mixture of Taoism and Buddhism).[48] Countries, such as China, often do not adhere to just one religion but practice both Confucianism and Taoism along with Buddhism.[49] In these situations, generally Taoist beliefs are followed for connection to the divine, Confucian beliefs are followed for moral conduct, and Buddhist beliefs are followed for the after-life.

Confucians follow five main traditions: (1) *Jen*: goodness of relations between people, (2) *Chun tzu*: each person should reflect humanity at its best, (3) *Li*: people cannot make wise decisions on their own but rather need to look to models for attention, (4) *Te*: people are ruled by power, such as governmental power, and (5) *Wen*: valuing peaceful arts, such as music and poetry.[50] Confucianism is often thought of as more of a code of ethics rather than a religion, although the teachings of Confucius reference heavenly support.[51] East Asian governments often like to encourage Confucius teachings because of the emphasis on following governmental ruling, and, in the past, Confucius teaching and governmental teachings have been seen as one and the same.[52]

Taoists are similar to Confucians in principles of moral behavior but differ in belief in Gods. There are two major groups in Taoism: religious Taoism and philosophical Taoism. As McDermott explains, religious Taoists "believe in gods with saving power, sinful human nature, and redemption from guilt and sin by means of prayer, penance, alchemy, and other rituals of personal religion."[53] In contrast, philosophical Taoists do not believe in a God or any kind of after-life and instead use the principles of Taoism to understand how the world operates.

How Confucianism/Taoism Influence Behavioral Economics

Businesses should avoid campaigns emphasizing self-assertiveness or competition because these behaviors are advised against in the Taoist sacred text, the *Tao Te Ching*.[54] Thus, any marketing communications or products that support these activities (e.g., competitive board games, empowerment and assertiveness self-help books, action movies) should not be targeted at devout Taoists. Confucians also follow a similar principle of righteousness where businesses should not encourage immoral behaviors (e.g., hurting others, violence, lying).[55] In contrast to this emphasis on avoiding self-assertiveness, Taoists honor those people who are weak and humble, such as disabled people. Thus, humanitarian aid programs could benefit from targeting Taoists for donations and volunteers.

Confucians follow a principle of reciprocity, similar to that of Christians—do not do unto others as you would not want done to yourself.[56] Thus, businesses desiring to bring about social change could encourage Confucians to act as they would want to be treated (e.g., anti-bullying campaigns, gun control practices, anti-smoking campaigns).

In addition, nature is to be loved and cared for in Taoist tradition.[57] Businesses selling sustainable products, pro-social behavior campaigns (e.g., recycling, composting), and nature conservancy charities would all benefit from targeting Taoists. These marketing practices should emphasize the universal caring for the environment.

The Chinese *yin/yang* symbol is a key component of Taoism, which businesses should understand. *Yin and Yang* represent the opposing forces of the world (e.g., good and evil, dark and light, life and death).[58] Placing this symbol in marketing communications could emphasize acceptance of the Taoist belief system. Many products and services are emblazoned with this symbol today with little respect for the symbol's roots in Taoism. If these currently existing products are marketed in communities with a high predominance of Taoism, then acknowledgement of the spirit of the Yin and Yang may increase sales and acceptance by Taoists.

In conclusion, many different perspectives characterize both Western and Eastern religions. We have presented big-picture differences, but of course many subtle differences also exist. Also, it is important to note that an individual person may modify the views of institutions, and, for some, spirituality and institutional religion are quite independent. Further, the differences in religion often co-vary with other differences—demographic, psychographic, and even geopolitical. For example, we have treated the differences between Catholics and Protestants from a theological perspective. One could also argue that quite apart from theology the differences between the two perspectives were in part driven by a geo-political desire to control the heart of Europe starting in the late Middle Ages.

CHAPTER 5

The Disconnect Between Belief Systems and Behavioral Economics

As evidenced in the prior chapters, all religious affiliations can influence consumer behaviors; however, the discussion of religion's influence on such behaviors is extremely limited, which is a detriment to the field of business.

As Bennis describes in a recent *Businessweek* report, business schools often put forward extensive effort to encourage "global mindsets," provide students with bilingual capabilities, promote study abroad opportunities, and offer international marketing courses.[1] However, what is missing from this "global mindset" is the influence of religion on business. As Bennis states, "… how can we educators claim credit for understanding, let alone teaching, the 'global mind' without a single course on the impact of religion on everyday life?"[2] Not only is there a dearth of discussion in business schools, but scholarly examination of religion's influence on behavioral economics is also lacking.

Sensitivity/Taboo Nature of "Religion"

Studies linking religiosity or religious affiliation to consumer behavior are quite limited,[3] with the exceptions often only assessing general religiosity or Western religious beliefs.[4] Comprehensive studies and a standardized expectation for study components are virtually nonexistent in the consumer behavior literature.[5] Most studies instead have measured related, but not directly applicable, dimensions in sociology, anthropology, psychology,[6] political science,[7] and economics.[8]

A possible explanation for this lack of research is the sensitivity of the religious subject that is considered taboo by many.[9] Lack of realization that religion can affect consumer behavior is another possible explanation where researchers only think religion affects the prominently studied areas of sociology, anthropology, and political science.[10] One study points to the availability of skilled interviewers who adhere to the religious customs of the area (e.g., only females are allowed to interview other females in Saudi Arabia) as a potential cause of this limited research.[11]

The lack of professors who are religious has also been identified as a reason for inadequate research relating religion to consumer behavior.[12] However, Gross and Simmons show that the majority of American professors are religious. About 67.5% of marketing professors believe in God, and 46.5% of those believing professors are certain that God exists without any doubt.[13] An additional 7% of marketing professors are spiritual, accounting for a total of 74.5% of marketing professors as either religious or spiritual.[14] Even across all types of educational institutions (elite doctoral, non-elite doctoral, four-year, and two-year), more professors are religious than not religious.[15] Therefore, blaming professors who do not believe in God for the lack of research is flawed reasoning.

Perhaps the diversity of religious perspectives, however, inhibits discussion about a topic that cannot be resolved "scientifically." The complexity nearly begs for resolution to conflicting beliefs that cannot be resolved through conventional scientific means. Scholars who seek simple solutions or "right" answers are often met with frustration.

Separation from Business

Religion is a key element of culture contributing to people's values and thereby influencing their behavior.[16] In fact, religion pervades society and influences both believers and non-believers.[17] For all its diversity and even inconsistency, it is a key source of inspiration for many people. From a macro perspective, religion influences the products and services on the market, the methods for marketing these products and services, and when and where these products and services are sold.[18]

Therefore, research addressing religion's influence on consumer behavior is important to businesses and vital for a comprehensive understanding of what causes consumers to behave as they do.[19] In addition, religiosity is an easily observable construct (as was detailed in the chapter on measuring religiosity) and therefore can be used by academics and practitioners alike.[20] To develop a strong base of religious influences on consumer and economic behavior, it is important to study religion and shopping behavior with the same level of rigor and objectivity as in other aspects of consumer behavior.[21]

Just as the *Businessweek* article at the beginning of this chapter described, many business schools will argue that religion should be kept as a distinctly different discipline from consumer behavior and business because it is not based on science. However, religion is a component of a consumer's core values in addition to being a key correlate of international identity. Thus, such a separation between religion and business only hinders business success. Even if religion is not derived from science, its consequences can be studied scientifically.

Costs to Business in Allowing this Separation to Continue

No matter what the reason for a lack of studies relating religion to consumer behavior, it is evident that businesses need to take action to understand religion. Companies should educate employees in international relations on the foundational beliefs of prominent religions in areas where the company operates. Businesses should examine customer segments to define core religious values and determine consumers' religiosity. Frontline service employees should be intimately aware of religious customs and directives in order to tailor conversations to the customer's religious views and to avoid the potential to offend the customer's beliefs.

If a company does not take steps to incorporate religious understanding into its business operations, the company risks offending a core customer base. For example, a simple advertisement encouraging consumers to enjoy the weekend with a glass of fine wine could greatly offend consumers who believe that drinking alcohol is forbidden by God. This offensive advertisement could lead the consumer to reject the brand and, especially in this age of social media, spread word of the company's actions across the globe in a matter of seconds. Understanding the customer's core values is more important today than ever before with the increase in international business, multicultural customer segments, and the ease with which social media may be used to either praise or blaze a company's actions.

CHAPTER 6

Comparing Belief Systems: Influences on Behavioral Economics

Although it is important to understand how specific religious affiliations influence consumer behavior, it is equally important to know how the behaviors of one religion compare to those of another. These comparisons become even more important when a business' target market is composed of a variety of religious groups, and the business needs to please and appeal to all religious groups. This chapter explores these interrelationships among religious affiliations as well as the influence of religiosity on consumer behavior. In particular, the behaviors in this chapter are explored from the perspective of academic research that has tested and validated the pivotal relationship between religious belief systems and behavioral economics.

This research examining the relationship between belief systems and behavioral economics is approached from the theoretical perspective of the values → attitudes → behavior hierarchy.[1] In this perspective, a consumer's core values lead to attitudes, such as attitudes that caring for society is critical or thoughts about sexual protection, that then lead to purchase behavior. These core values are rooted in religious views that are derived from religious scriptures and teachings. These values then influence attitudes. With these attitudes cemented in the consumer's mind, consumers then (often) participate in behaviors that are consistent with these attitudes, such as donating money to societal charities or buying products that are consistent with the teachings of scriptures.[2] This values → attitudes → behavior hierarchy is critically important for understanding how a consumer's religious values lead to differences in consumption behavior and behavioral economics.

Overview

The first academic research study investigating religion and consumer behavior was conducted by Engel in 1976.[3] However, one study by Thompson and Raine[4] assessing religiosity and store preference was published in the same year as Engel's work.[5] These two works constitute the beginnings of the religion and consumer behavior topic, although they are not necessarily foundational or seminal works. That seminal/foundational status is given to Wilkes, Burnett, and Howell[6], Hirschman[7], Bailey and Sood[8], Sood and Nasu[9], McDaniel and Burnett [10], LaBarbera[11], and Delener[12]. These authors, whose papers we will discuss in more detail later, provide a more conceptual understanding of why consumers' religious affiliation and level of religiosity leads to differences in consumer behavior.

The results of the research on religion and consumer behavior thus far show that religion has the ability to influence consumer behavior in two main ways: directly through explicit prohibitions in religious books and by religious leaders (e.g., *halal* or *kosher* foods) or indirectly through the values that are impressed upon by the religious group.[13] In addition, religion has the ability to influence the marketplace in four forms: political authority (e.g., religious government control prohibiting TV commercials), institutional authority (e.g. the church prohibiting members from consuming alcohol), social authority (e.g., through cultural beliefs and values), and competitive authority (e.g., religious groups competing with one another).[14]

Apart from these marketplace authorities, religion can also influence consumer behavior in a variety of ways, including ceremonial guidelines, suggested gender roles, and adherence to religious holidays.[15] In spite of the numerous ways that religion influences consumer behavior, the topic of religion is only very gradually infiltrating business education in the form of a paragraph or a few pages at the most in consumer behavior textbooks.[16] Although education may be quiet on the topic of religion, many companies are taking steps to incorporate religion into business operations including Pfizer, Merck, Smucker's, several auto companies, and Tyson.[17] For example, Tyson offers downloadable prayer books on its website for religious consumers to use while consuming Tyson products.[18]

Tyson's chief marketing officer explains that Tyson's values are to be a faith-friendly company, which is especially important given that the majority of Americans (and consumers around the world) are religious. Tyson feels that by providing religious-related materials on its website, it is better living out its values and connecting with religious consumers. Other companies incorporate religion into business through scriptural reference on product packaging (e.g., Forever 21), banning pay-per-view pornography in hotel rooms (e.g., Marriott Company), creating religious advertisements (e.g., Hobby Lobby), not promoting alcohol consumption (e.g., George Foreman products), or donating revenues to anti-abortion causes (e.g., Curves).[19] If many corporations and practitioners find religion useful in understanding consumer behavior, why are academics and business undergraduate and graduate education lagging behind in assessing religion's usefulness in predicting behavior in the marketplace? Refer back to the previous chapter on the disconnect between belief systems and behavioral economics for several reasons why religion is slow to gain attention in consumer behavior research.

A framework developed by the authors of *Consumption and Spirituality* categorizes the interaction between consumer behavior and spirituality into four categories: (1) sacralization of the mundane (i.e., sacred meaning is added to an ordinary object, such as school gym becoming a place for religious service), (2) spiritual meanings in consumption (i.e., how consumption becomes sacred, such as collecting), (3) commodification of the spiritual (i.e., marketing religious services, such as churches marketing to attract new members), and (4) consumption of spiritual goods (i.e., purchasing religious goods, such as a cross necklace).[20] These categories provide a good starting place to understand how religion can influence consumption. However, one more category should be added— (5) adapting to the sacred. This additional category describes ways in which businesses understand and adapt to the religious needs of consumers, such as changing ingredients to be *kosher* or changing advertising to adapt to religious moral standards.

Although religion and consumer behavior research is generally lacking, there are several researchers who have stepped into this topic to examine this very interesting relationship. For example, Kahle and colleagues have investigated religion's influence on consumer values.[21] These authors explain that one of the basic components of religion is values, which are shown to differ based on religion and religious intensity.[22] Buddhists are most likely to value warm relations and being respected. Taoists value being respected and self-fulfillment. Muslims and Hindus especially value self-respect and security. Christians value warm relations and self-respect. Agnostics and atheists value warm relations and self-fulfillment most.[23] This emphasis on self-respect for Muslims, Hindus, and Christians correlates with scriptural emphasis on acting in a way that is ethical and respectable by God or other divine being. In contrast, Taoists, agnostics, and atheists value self-fulfillment, which is celebration of personal success, an area where the highly religious are instructed to make attributions to and thank God for successes. Values, based on the list of values (LOV), are shown to influence service activity consumption as well.[24] Thus, Buddhists may be more interested in purchasing a product or participating in a service that allows them to increase warm relationships with others (e.g., purchasing party food), while Hindus would prefer to have a product or service that increases self-respect (e.g., a language learning course).

Belief Systems and Ethics

One of the most prominently studied areas relating to religion and consumer behavior involves ethics, with many studies in both the consumer behavior and psychology literature. Religion can influence ethics through individual religious beliefs as well as the religion of the surrounding environment.[25] For example, a Taoist in America is going to be influenced by personal Taoist beliefs but also by Christian beliefs since Christianity is the predominant religion in America. Because many religious scriptures dictate ethical behavior (e.g., do not steal, do unto others as you want them to do unto you), much of ethics is rooted in religion. Hunt and Vitell argue that any theory of marketing ethics should incorporate religion.[26]

Different religions have varying views of what constitutes ethical and unethical behavior[27] with research showing that Christians are more accepting of borderline behaviors compared to Muslims, Buddhists, Hindus, and Confucianists.[28] Other research shows that internally religious consumers (i.e., those that have an internal relationship with a divine being) are more likely to regard questionable consumer behaviors as unethical in comparison to externally religious consumers (e.g., those that go to church, wear religious clothing, or otherwise are primarily religious only in ways that are seen by others).[29]

Another study found Buddhists to be the most relativist (moral standards are individualistic) and Muslims and southern Christians to be the most idealist (moral standards are clear-cut and should always be followed).[30] Thus, religious doctrine for Muslims and southern Christians would act as an ethical standard, while Buddhists would seek a personal, individualized understanding of ethics. Nationality is also found to influence ethical views, signifying a need to separate national influences from religious influences on consumer behavior.[31] For example, Brazilians may feel that not stopping at stop signs is acceptable for safety reasons whereas Americans feel that it is not. To get around these national differences, it is beneficial to examine how religious groups differ within a country rather than across countries. Thus, every person would be influenced by the same culture and any differences between religious groups would be due to differences in religion rather than differences in culture.

Ethical values can also lead to views about what is controversial and should be marketed with caution. For example, one study shows that many Muslims view gender/sex related products, health and care products, and addictive products as significantly more controversial than Buddhists, Christians, and consumers who are not religious.[32] Across all religious affiliations, highly religious consumers (as opposed to less or not religious consumers) are the most likely to find sexual appeals in advertising offensive, which is expected given the emphasis against lusting in religious scriptures.[33] According to another study, no differences between religions exist in viewing social/political groups as controversial.[34] In addition, a study on fair trade products (i.e., products certified to respect the producers and origin of a product's suppliers) shows that some religious consumers consider fair trade products to be an ethical matter. For example, Buddhists are shown to be the most likely of all the major religions to purchase fair trade products.[35] This result goes back to references to caring for humankind in the sacred text.

Belief Systems and Consumer Behavior

At this point, it is clear that religion influences consumer and economic behavior. Religion is definitely an understudied, yet essential, component of an accurate picture of consumer behavior. In addition, the studies that do examine purchasing behavior and decision making find significant differences between religious groups. For example, one study finds that Jewish consumers are more innovative and are more apt to be opinion leaders than all other religious affiliations (Catholic, Protestant, Hindu, Muslim, Buddhist).[36] In another study on innovation, Catholics are found to be more innovative in dancing, transportation options, and sports, while Protestants are more innovative with religious ideas and hair styles.[37] Jewish consumers are viewed as more innovative than Christians because of Jews being encouraged to seek knowledge individually within the synagogue. In addition, Catholics are more likely to be opinion leaders than Jews or Protestants when choosing dances, places to shop, political ideas, religious ideas, and sports.[38] Hindus are also more innovative and ethnically conscious than Muslims, Buddhists, and Christians.[39] This research is correlational in nature, though, and further research is needed to explore why consumers of these religious affiliations are more innovative in certain categories than other religious affiliations.

Political attitudes differ based on Protestant denominations as well.[40] For example, American Baptist (AB) clergy are 62% conservative, whereas the Evangelical Lutheran Church of America (ELCA) clergy is only 22% conservative. In another study, Protestants and Hindus were shown as more likely to be supportive of income inequality in exchange for incentives than other religious groups.[41] Not only are there political differences between religions, but differences also exist in consumption amounts. In a study on soda consumption, Catholics were shown to consume more soda than Protestants.[42] Although this is correlational research and not strongly linked to religious doctrine, these differences do exist which businesses should be aware of.

As discussed in the chapters on Western and Eastern religions, religious groups differ in perspectives on gender roles. For example, Muslims place more emphasis on traditional family roles and fashion conservativeness than Buddhists, Hindus, and Christians.[43] It would be expected that gender roles (i.e., husband works, wife cares for the kids and house) and conservative dressing (i.e., the *hijab* or *burqa* for Muslims—although it is debated whether the *burqa* is a result of religious or cultural customs) go hand in hand given that these are both based in Islamic scripture. In another interesting study, traditional Muslims, who hold to traditional gender roles are more likely to purchase whole fresh chicken over cut or frozen chicken.[44] In contrast, orthodox Jews, who do not strictly follow traditional gender roles, are more likely to buy frozen whole or cut chicken.[45] The reasoning behind this preference for chicken rests on the time to prepare the chicken at home (i.e., a wife at home can prepare whole chicken, a wife who is working outside the home has little time and needs pre-cut chicken).

Muslims are also shown to be different from consumers following other religious groups in terms of shopping behavior. For example, Muslims are more likely to rank merchandise, reputation and price as extremely important store attributes, whereas Hindus find attractiveness to be a more important store attribute.[46] Muslims prefer shopping at hypermarkets and through catalogs more than other religions, whereas Hindus prefer department stores, specialty departments, or specialty stores in comparison to other religions.[47] The Hindu's focus on shopping in specialty stores could be a result of searching for products that are made by Hindu specification (i.e., no beef). In terms of shopping day, Protestants are more likely to believe that nonessential business should be closed on Sundays with Catholics following a close second.[48] This is in line with the Bible stating that God rested on the seventh day of creation, which many today interpret to be Sunday. In another study of consumers in both the United States and Japan, highly religious Protestants are more likely to buy products when they are on sale rather than when they need them, and they are more willing to buy foreign products.[49] This finding is a business challenge for local manufacturers who are more expensive than foreign manufacturers and whose competitive advantage is the local production.

In terms of other shopping behaviors, Catholics are also found to be more thoughtful, traditional, and demanding when purchasing a TV compared to Hindus, whereas Muslims are more practical and innovative.[50] The traditional focus of Catholics could be rooted in their emphasis on traditions and rituals in the church. Essoo and Dibb identify seven segments that religious consumers can fall into: demanding shopper, practical shopper, trendy shopper, traditional shopper, economic shopper, thoughtful shopper, and innovative shopper.[51] Consumers can also be segmented based on generational group into baby boomers (i.e., consumers in their 40s–60s) and generation Y consumers (i.e., consumers in their teens–30s). Research findings show generation Y consumers to be less religious and more materialistic.[52] However, other research shows that teachings from the church have a greater influence on materialistic desires for younger consumers than older consumers.[53] Associating traditional segmentation variables (e.g., age) with religious affiliation and religiosity levels, such as the previous study suggests, could assist businesses in incorporating religion into currently existing target markets.

Religious affiliation has also been found to influence sustainable consumption. Consumers of Christian denominations, who believe that the Bible is the infallible word of God, are less likely to hold sustainable consumption attitudes (e.g., believing that caring for the environment is good) or participate in sustainable consumption behaviors (e.g., recycle, purchase organic fruits and vegetables) in comparison to consumers of Christian denominations who believe that the Bible should be interpreted in light of current times.[54] These differences are hypothesized because of Christian consumers' belief that God gave man control over nature (e.g., naming animals) and that the world has a true end point leading some Christians to feel that spreading the news of Christianity is more important than caring for the environment. Other studies, conversely, show little to no effect of religious affiliation on sustainable consumption attitudes and behaviors.[55] However, recent sustainability movements within the church are changing these views. For further discussion on religion and sustainability, read the case on *Religion and Sustainable Public Policy* in Chapter 9.

Different religious affiliations also have significantly different service behaviors. For example, in the broader area of consumer behavior, very few studies in the tourism industry have looked at the effects of religion on tourist behavior.[56] When visiting the Wailing Wall, a religious tourist monument in Israel, Jews were more likely than Christians and agnostics or atheists to be moved emotionally and to evoke a sense of pride.[57]

Jews also differed significantly from Christians in reasons for visiting the Wailing Wall. Jews visited the site more because of its religious characteristics, the physical nature of the site, a desire for entertainment, and because of a sense of belonging.[58] Alternatively, Christians visited the Wailing Wall more because it was on the way to another site, a desire to learn more about the site, and because it was a world famous site.[59] Christian tourists in Israel, on the other hand, are more likely to be moved by Jordan River baptismal sites or the location of Jesus' Sermon on the Mount, both of which hold more significance for Christian believers.

Religious groups also differ in terms of brand loyalty. Religious fundamentalism (e.g., liberal vs. conservative believers) influences brand commitment with Buddhist and Christian fundamentalists being more brand loyal when asked about cell phones and wristwatches.[60] Another study shows that fundamentalists are more likely to be brand loyal, whereas highly spiritual consumers are less likely to be brand loyal.[61] Perhaps loyalty to one's religious group also correlates with loyalty in other aspects of life, such as brand commitment. Religiosity could also be considered a substitute for brand reliance. Research shows that consumers who are more religious are less likely to desire branded goods for items contributing highly to self-worth.[62] In other words, brand loyalty is low for goods that are purely designed to enhance the self rather than foster a spirit of giving to others or worshipping God.

In spite of a handful of studies questioning the ability of religiosity to predict consumer behavior, numerous studies show significant relations between religiosity and consumer behavior.[63] Consumers of higher religiosity are more likely to perceive greater risk in purchase decisions[64] and to have the husband be the primary decider of household purchase decisions in comparison to agnostics and atheists.[65] In another study, casually religious consumers (compared to devoutly religious) are shown to be trendier, more innovative, more practical, and more demanding when making television-related purchasing decisions.[66] Highly religious consumers are also more likely to accept the traditional gender roles, more likely to have higher life satisfaction, and more likely to be opinion leaders.[67] These findings follow suit with research in psychology showing that religious individuals are happier and less stressed in part owing to their ability to pass their concerns along to God.

Religiosity is also predictive of shopping behavior. For example, consumers who are more religious are slightly less likely to purchase genetically modified meats as compared to less religious consumers but to such a small extent that genetic modification is not considered an ethical or moral issue.[68] Consumers with higher levels of religiosity are also more likely to be trendy shoppers preferring high quality goods and well-known brands. More specifically, this study showed that highly religious consumers preferred high quality, existing brands of cell phones in comparison to less religious consumers.[69] As expected, another study on shopping behavior showed that highly religious Muslims were less likely to purchase the taboo product of soda than less religious Muslims.[70] Across religious groups, it would be expected that consumers of higher religiosity would be more likely to follow scriptural mandates (e.g., do not drink alcohol, avoid lustful products).

Just as Allport and Ross identified the difference between intrinsically and extrinsically religious individuals, studies have found differences between intrinsically and extrinsically religious consumers.[71] Consumers who are high on intrinsic religiosity (e.g., personal connection with God) are more likely to be quality conscious, impulsive, and less price conscious than consumers low on intrinsic religiosity, even after controlling for demographic variables.[72] In contrast, consumers who are high on extrinsic religiosity (e.g., religious service attendance, purchase of religious goods) are more likely to be quality conscious (just as with internally religious consumers), less impulsive, and more price conscious than low externally religious consumers.[73] These findings make sense given that externally religious consumers are often more concerned with how they appear to others and thus more conscious about the decisions they make (low impulsivity, highly watchful of prices). However, a consumer could be high on both intrinsic and extrinsic religiosity, thus the findings from this study refer mostly to those individuals who are high on one dimension of religiosity and low on the other dimension.

Religiosity is important not only for product or service manufacturers but is important to all involved in the marketing process, including retail stores. A study on evaluation of retail stores shows that consumers who internalize religion are more likely to evaluate retail stores based on shopping efficiency, friendliness of sales personnel, and product quality.[74] Yet highly religious consumers are less likely to be store loyal and are more apt to voice complaints than less religious consumers.[75] However, Choi finds that highly religious consumers are actually more store loyal,[76] and switching behavior (whether at the store or brand level) is reduced for more religious consumers but unaffected by religious affiliation.[77] Clearly, research addressing religion's effects on store loyalty and switching behavior is insufficient and therefore inconclusive.

Also of interest to retail stores is where and when religious consumers prefer to shop. One study shows that highly religious individuals spend fewer Sundays shopping, spend less money on Sundays, and are more likely to believe that all nonessential business should be closed on Sundays.[78] Another study shows that highly spiritual consumers are more likely to inshop (shop in town rather than out of town).[79] An interesting future study might test this idea with the current generation and look at the tendency to shop online with relation to religiosity and religious affiliation.[80] A study discussed earlier mentioned that Protestants (with no reference to religiosity) are more willing to purchase foreign goods. This raises a challenge with much research examining religion and religiosity— only religion or religiosity are measured, not both. There is a delicate interaction between religion and religiosity. Businesses need to assess both to get an accurate understanding of a target market and of how this target market's belief system influences consumer behavior.

Continuing with studies specifically addressing religiosity, it is important for businesses selling both goods and services to understand consumers' religiosity. In a study of the tourism industry, highly religious consumers were more apt to think a tourism experience was educational, emotionally moving, heritage related, and filled with pride.[81] These feelings of pride could be due to highly religious consumers crediting God or other religious beings for the environment of their destination. In addition, often tourist experiences are marketed with a religious theme, whether it be a daily prayer session, a visit to religiously-significant places, or even a pilgrimage.

Occasionally, no difference or mixed differences are found between varying religiosity levels and consumer behaviors. For example, one study showed that a consumer's level of religiosity is not significantly correlated with materialism,[82] although other research suggests that spirituality (not necessarily religiosity) is highly correlated with materialism.[83] Yet another study suggests that the relationship between religion and materialism is dependent upon culture and the amount of television viewing.[84] In another study, where only Protestant, Catholic, Jew, or no religious affiliation were assessed, religious affiliation was found not to influence retail store evaluative criteria.[85] In a different study assessing purchase of specific goods, no difference was found between Catholics and Protestants in purchase of air travel, beer, blue jeans, eating at restaurants, shampoo, movie theatre attendance, or stereo set purchases. However, no measure of religiosity or expansion beyond the two basic religious groups (i.e., Catholic, Protestant) was used in this study. Thus, religion cannot be completely ruled out of purchase decisions involving each of these activities and products.[86] Because these studies assessing religion and consumer behavior are all exploratory, non-significant differences are inconclusive, and all findings need to be replicated. Thus, these non-significant findings may be more due to measurement error and lack of connecting purchase behaviors with theory. For example, one could ask, why would Catholics and Protestants be different in their purchase of stereo sets?

In addition to these issues, the change in church fundamentalism is important to consider when reviewing studies many years apart. Distinctions between what is sacred (e.g., religious books) and what is profane (e.g., alcohol) are changing. Some religious groups are becoming more lenient in this distinction, and others are returning to fundamental beliefs in religious doctrine.[87]

As a final note on religion and consumer behavior, studies show that age,[88] education,[89] and marital status[90] can interact with religion when assessing shopping behavior. However, another study shows that education is not significantly related to religious commitment.[91] In general, these studies show that consumers who are older, less educated (though depends greatly on religious affiliation), and married are more likely to be religious. Interactions between religion and gender[92] or religion and income[93] are not significant. However, one study finds a positive relation between gender and religion where females are more religious than males.[94]

Marketing Belief Systems

In addition to the influence of religion on consumer behavior in the marketing of secular products, religion also influences the market for religious goods and services. Research shows that marketing of religious products has been on the rise recently.[95] The market for Christian products in particular is a multibillion-dollar-per-year industry,[96] and it encompasses everything from clothing to education to music.[97] There are even organizations devoted specifically to Christian businesses, such as the Christian Businessmen's Committee United States of America and the Full Gospel Businessmen's Fellowship.[98] In addition, with the rise of the evangelical market segment, the market for religious goods has increased.[99] However, literature related to marketing religious products is very limited and is most often restricted to the religion literature.[100]

One of the easiest ways for a company to target a religious audience would be to add a religious symbol to advertising. However, studies have shown mixed results for the effectiveness of religious symbols in advertising. With highly religious and highly involved consumers, the Christian cross has been proven to increase positive attitudes toward the advertisement, but with less involved but still highly religious consumers, the cross decreases attention to the advertisement.[101] Highly religious consumers also view Christian symbols more positively in advertising when the symbol is associated with the advertised item, but they view the advertisement negatively when the item is unrelated to the religious symbol.[102] Dotson and Hyatt suggest careful consideration when using religious symbols in advertising to understand the associations that might be made between the religious symbol and the advertised item, as well as how the sacred object is portrayed in the advertisement.[103]

The use of Christian religious symbols in advertisements is on the rise but understudied in the literature.[104] Advertisements in Yellow Pages that use Christian religious symbols showed significantly different attitude toward the advertisements based on consumers' religiosity. Highly religious Christians are more likely to look favorably on the use of Christian religious symbols (e.g., the *ichthus*, often understood as the fish symbol) in advertising, have greater purchase intentions, and higher perceived product quality for the product/service with the Christian symbol.[105] Before immediately deciding to use Christian symbols in advertising, however, businesses should understand that using the symbol may heighten customer expectations for the product or company.[106]

In a study on recall of religious advertisements, Andeleeb showed that recall and preference for hospitals with a religious affiliation were greater for patients who had similar religious beliefs.[107] However, when explicitly asked for factors that contribute to choosing a hospital, respondents listed the hospital's religious affiliation as low in importance. This finding suggests that religious businesses should convey religious beliefs in addition to the businesses' strategic advantages when the targeted audience has the same religious affiliation as the business. Also, these results show that consumers are often unaware of what influences their decision making (e.g., unaware of the great influence that religious affiliation has).

Religious businesses benefit from the desire of consumers to experience the sacred through consumption.[108] In other words, consumers adhere to their religious beliefs by buying a Bible, meditation mat, religious jewelry and so forth. Belk and colleagues identify six main sacred consumer domains: places, times, tangible things, intangibles, persons, and experiences.[109] For example, a religious temple is a sacred place that can be marketed as a tourism destination.

Christmas and Hanukkah are times during the year that are sacred and provide opportunities for religious businesses to sell products or holiday-related gifts (although some people would argue this secularization of the sacred is a negative trend in religious consumption). Holiday-related retail sales in the United States accounted for $579.8 billion in 2012, which is an increase of 3% from 2011.[110] These sales can represent anywhere from 20%–40% of a business' total sales for the year, which warrants attention from any business and highlights the importance of understanding religious holidays. Businesses need to be increasingly attuned to the online environment as sales online are increasing every year and estimated to have been over $90 billion in 2012. Not only are sales changing during the holiday season, but businesses are hiring many additional part-time employees to handle increased demand. In fact, over 600,000 part-time employees have been hired in previous years during the holiday season. In addition to being creative with advertising to recognize the religious importance of holidays while not offending religious groups with other beliefs, businesses may consider offering faith-based products. There are many tangible objects that can be used to express faith, such as jewelry, faith-based posters, books, picture frames with a religious message, or bumper stickers for the car. Any type of gifting during this season, however, can represent observation of religious tradition. The case study *Best Buy and Holiday Advertising* in Chapter 9 further explores a business' operations during the holiday season and examines how to appropriately acknowledge each religion's holiday celebrations.

Referring back to Belk and colleagues' description of sacred objects, an object can become sacred in one of seven ways: ritual, pilgrimage, quintessence (e.g., Swiss army knife being the sacred representation of Switzerland), gift-giving, collecting, inheritance, or external sanction (e.g., placing an item in a museum).[111] For example, a secular gift given as a present during confirmation (a Catholic event where a teenager confirms his or her faith in the church) would become sacred because it was given during a sacred time. This can apply outside of religious faith too. For example, people who collect sports paraphernalia feel the items are sacred and cannot get rid of them.

Not all religious individuals, however, support consumption of the sacred. Religious individuals can be separated into nonusers of sacred consumption (e.g., "Jesus wouldn't buy the t-shirt") and users of sacred consumption (e.g., need for belonging, desire to spread the religious message, excited by their religious spirit).[112] Examples such as the religious theme park, Heritage Village, suggest that consumption and materialism among religious individuals is becoming more acceptable.[113]

Religious organizations, such as churches, are also competitive forces in the marketplace and often face conflict between holding true to religious values and being competitive with other religious organizations.[114] For example, small denominational churches that do not do anything to market the church can dwindle as churches that emphasize door-to-door invites, mailings, and posters around town increase in size because of marketing efforts.

Marketing faith is on the rise, but businesses need to be cautious to control brand reputation. Branding can help establish (or re-establish) a religious group's identity.[115] In the past few years, there have been several attempts at rebranding religious groups in an effort to create a more positive brand image for the group. For example, the "I am a Mormon" campaign featured TV, radio, and print advertisements along with an Internet marketing campaign to show that Mormons are similar to other people.

This campaign has helped increase awareness of the Mormon religion and improved their brand image. Another similar campaign came out featuring Muslims in America with the "Inspired by Mohammad" campaign.

Thus, religion influences behavioral economics and consumer behavior from a variety of angles. Religious consumers are influenced by religious scriptures and religious leaders, which lead to different shopping behaviors for secular goods. In addition, religious consumers have created a market for sacred goods along with religious institutions themselves being a marketed service. As competition across markets increase, businesses would greatly benefit from looking to religion to better understand and target consumers.

CHAPTER 7

Comparing Belief Systems: Influences on Consumers

Although the research on religion and consumer behavior is limited, the field of psychology has much more research on religion and general behaviors. This chapter explores some of the key findings from this research in psychology and provides discussion on how these general behaviors lead to differences in consumer behavior and influence the field of behavioral economics.

Similar to the previous chapter on religion, consumer behavior, and behavioral economics, the values → attitudes → behaviors hierarchy plays a critical role in understanding the relationship between religion and psychological behavior. Again, religious values that are derived from religious scriptures and teachings influence core attitudes, which then influence health behaviors, risky behaviors, social interactions, and many other psychology-related behaviors. As previously stated, each of these behaviors has consumption implications. For example, religion is found to correlate with increased health, which leads to less consumption of health procedures. With each of the behaviors described below, the consumption practices are driven by religious values and important for businesses to understand.

Overview

Before delving into the specific religion and psychology research, it is beneficial to review how psychologists view religion and the general status of psychology of religion research. Some psychologists believe that religion is a result of the way our brains work in an effort to account for the chaos in the world.[1] Others believe that it is a mechanism to transmit cultural social control. Yet another view sees religion as the source of a sense of security for facing the unknown status of human consciousness after death. Regardless of the reason individuals are religious, it is clear through a plethora of research that religion influences human behavior. In a comprehensive literature review in the field of the psychology of religion, Emmons and Paloutzian identify that research addressing the psychological aspects of religion is still sparse, although it has grown significantly in the last 25 years.[2] However, in comparison to the research on religion and consumer behavior, the research on the psychology of religion is plentiful. The taboo nature of religion in science is also cited as the reason for the lack of research in the psychology of religion, which is the same reason suggested for a lack of studies addressing behavioral economics and religion.[3]

The establishment of a division of the American Psychological Association (APA) on the Psychology of Religion and Spirituality in 1976 has assisted in increasing research in the psychology of religion field.[4] Possibly, if such a similar division were created in business, this organization could help to increase the literature assessing how religion influences consumer behavior.

Literature addressing the psychology of religion is most often found in the Journal for the Scientific Study of Religion; Review of Religious Research; The International Journal for the Psychology of Religion (created in 1990); Mental Health, Religion, and Culture; and Research in the Social Scientific Study of Religion.[5] Organizations are also realizing the importance of addressing spirituality in the workplace, adding spiritual consultants as part of the work force to assist with creating mind-body awareness.[6] Spirituality, a key component of religion, is significantly different from the "big five" or the five-factor model of personality (i.e., openness, conscientiousness, extraversion, agreeableness, neuroticism), implying the importance of spirituality in a comprehensive understanding of consumer personality.[7]

Religion and Health

Numerous studies show the health benefits of devoted religiousness.[8] More specifically, research shows that religious people are less depressed, have higher morals, exhibit lower levels of drug and alcohol abuse, and live longer.[9] Active churchgoers are also more tender-minded, have higher super ego strength, exhibit lower levels of dominance, and are more conservative.[10] In addition, individuals who are more religious tend to have greater overall well-being even after controlling for all basic demographic variables.[11] Whereas agnostics and atheists could seek out counselors, drugs, or alcohol to deal with problems, religious consumers could turn to a god or religious being to seek help with problems (in addition to the aforementioned options). Stress is reduced through activities such as prayer, which can contribute to greater overall well-being. Each of these factors contributes to greater overall healthiness, leading to a somewhat lower need for healthcare, mental health treatment, and prescription drugs. At the same time, because religious people live longer and tend to be somewhat more conservative, religious consumers have a higher customer lifetime value for brands (i.e., more years to buy a brand and exhibit brand loyalty).

In addition, internally religious individuals are happier and have greater life satisfaction according to studies of both United States and Singapore residents.[12] However, externally religious individuals only have greater happiness and life satisfaction for United States residents.[13] Sincerely happy people see religion as reflecting who they are rather than the activities in which they participate.[14] Also, religious individuals are more likely to be pro-social, leading to less aggression, higher altruism, and higher empathy, after controlling for gender.[15] This greater desire for pro-social behaviors in general is beneficial for pro-social businesses to understand. Religious consumers can represent the core target market for a pro-social company. This emphasis on pro-social behavior is rooted in religious scriptures where adherents are encouraged to do good to others to express their beliefs or to be rewarded in heaven, a future life, nirvana, or other end time.

Also of interest to businesses, other research shows that religious people tend to be less materialistic. This observation means that religious people often do not find happiness in things but rather find happiness in worshipping a religious deity, relationships, and other psychological activities. Well-being is negatively associated with materialism in highly religious individuals, indicating that religiously zealous individuals feel the pressure to be less materialistic and feel conflict when materialistic desires occur.[16] This conflict between spirituality and internal religiosity, on the one hand, and materialism, on the other, stems from Plato's distinction between the body and soul (i.e., between material objects and the non-material spiritual aspects of life).[17] As religious individuals seek to be less materialistic, advertisers should be cautious in marketing goods or services that are strictly self-promoting or status symbols to religious individuals. Rather, businesses should focus on the specific purpose of goods and services to emphasize the need for the good or service and help decrease materialistic conflicts for religious consumers.

Religion and Morality

As discussed in the previous chapter on religion and ethics in consumer behavior, much research in psychology shows a strong connection between highly religious individuals and moral behavior. Although there are entire academic journals and fields of psychology devoted to religion and ethical behavior, the discussion here will be limited because of the prior discussion on religion and consumer ethics that is more relevant to the topic of this book.

In general, studies show that individual personality differs based on religiosity and religious orientation (whether intrinsic or extrinsic).[18] More specifically, intrinsically religious individuals are more likely to have strong moral standards, be conscientious, well mannered, responsible, consistent, sensitive, and empathetic.[19] Extrinsically religious individuals, agnostics, and atheists have similar personality characteristics of being flexible, self-reliant, skeptical, orderly, and less emotional.[20]

These findings would be expected given the moral standards provided in religious doctrine (e.g., the Ten Commandments, care for the planet, treat others as you want to be treated). Businesses should take note not to encourage behaviors that are considered immoral to the religious group being targeted. In addition, companies and non-profits that specialize in promoting moral behaviors (e.g., caring for the environment, caring for one's parents) would perhaps benefit from targeting religious individuals in view of the heightened focus on moral actions.

Religion and Risky Behaviors

Religion also influences one's desire to participate in risky activities. For example, a study on risky behavior in college students shows that both

Catholic and Protestant college students are less likely to choose a spring break destination based on the ease of access to alcohol and drugs. These religious college students are also less likely overall to use drugs during spring break.[21] Thus, spring break party destinations (e.g., Cancun, Mexico; Miami Beach, Florida; Las Vegas, Nevada; Nassau, Bahamas) should be cautious targeting religious individuals and religious communities.

Religion also influences the riskiness of general purchase behaviors. For example, research shows that Muslims are more impulsive yet less risky shoppers.[22] In addition, Catholics perceive more risk when making purchase decisions in comparison to Jews.[23] This difference in risky shopping behavior could lead a Muslim or Catholic to be less likely than a Jew to purchase products from unknown brands or new products where the risks are higher of the product not performing as advertised.

Risky behavior is influenced by one's level of religiosity just as it is by one's religious affiliation. Highly religious females are less likely to consume alcohol and to participate in risky sexual behavior than less religious females.[24] These findings follow the doctrine of many religious affiliations that strongly advise against pre-marital sex. With regards to ethics, the more religious a consumer is, the more likely he or she will be idealistic (making decisions based on moral rules) and less relativistic (using personal judgment as a moral guide).[25] Similar to pre-marital sex, highly religious consumers are more likely to base decisions on religious doctrine, which would lead to these more idealistic views of ethics. For example, a highly religious consumer may be more likely to look to religious scripture that says "do not steal" and follow that prescription. Instead, a less religious consumer may be more apt to make a personal judgment and think that his or her current low income means that it is okay to steal or lie on tax forms.

Interestingly, the relation between risky behaviors (alcohol consumption and risky sexual behavior) is inconclusive for a male sample.[26] However, a student sample was used for the study; thus, this study should be replicated with a general population sample before reaching a generalized conclusion. Thus, in general, religious doctrine and religious leaders provide prescriptions on moral behavior leading highly religious individuals to participate less in risky behaviors in comparison to less religious or not religious individuals.

Religion and Social Networks

Religion can serve as a foundation for building a social identity, which is then associated with social networks.[27] These social networks exist as in-person groups and online groups (e.g., Facebook, Twitter) that provide businesses with highly targetable market segments. Research shows that a significant element of many religions is these social networks of support and friends with similar values.[28] In addition, religions establish role expectations (e.g., fundamental religions portraying the woman as the bearer of children), which help create one's social identity.[29] Interest in consumer identity has increased in recent years, but businesses must ask,—"What is the source of a consumer's identity?" Religion is a key component of a consumer's identity, especially for highly religious consumers, and thus is important for businesses to understand.

Social identity theory purports that a person gains perception of his or her self through the perceptions of others.[30] For example, consumers may be more likely to participate in religious groups in an effort to be perceived by others as religious individuals. This recognition is similar to the concept of external religiosity where consumers participate in publicly visible religious behaviors, possibly because of a desire to be seen by others as being religious. External religiosity is also similar to one of the basic human values included in the List of Values (LOV): sense of belonging. This sense of belonging is associated with church affiliation and church attendance, with Protestants being the most likely to exhibit this value.[31] Again, referring back to Allport and Ross's distinction between intrinsic and extrinsic religiosity, social identity theory and religious social networks generally describe the external dimension of religiosity.[32]

Some psychologists cite these social networks as part of the reason religion in some places stays strong today[33] and why it is difficult for individuals to leave a religion.[34] Religious organizations provide social support to members, providing help in times of crisis and appreciation in times of success. Religious communities are much more than just associations; instead, they represent theological social connections.[35] Many religions use the social aspects of their religious community as a tool to retain current members and to attract new members because humans desire to belong.[36] Thus, anyone involved in marketing religion should emphasize the social connection opportunities within the faith communities to ful-fill the individual's basic need for a sense of belonging. For businesses selling non-religious goods, emphasizing how products or services can be used within a group of friends (e.g., a religious community group) may increase desire for the items.

Though understudied, a potential source of insight for businesses would be the influence that these social networks have on consumer choice of products and services. Choi and colleagues suggest that religious social groups can influence members' thoughts and opinions regarding products.[37] For example, if a member of a religious community talks about how much he or she liked a movie seen in the theater the previous night, other members of the community will be more inclined to see this movie. Other research confirms that religious social groups along with religious norms influence consumption decisions.[38] These consumption decisions in turn help an individual to create and recognize his or her religious identity.[39] Social media have multiplied the group connections among religious communities in recent years. In any case, consumption and religious identity are tightly intertwined, making it important for businesses to assess the religious identity of target markets.

Religious groups provide members not only with basic life norms but also with images of appropriate life roles.[40] Because religious groups rep-resent such a foundational role in life, another potential area for study is how businesses can adequately target a specific religious group and market their product within a religious social group, although businesses should be cautious if marketing directly to a religious social group so as not to be seen purely as a persuasive advertising attempt. Interestingly, Buddhists have lower levels of religious identity in comparison to Taoists, Muslims, Hindus, and Christians.[41] Therefore, businesses should under-stand differences between religious affiliations and the affiliation's impor-tance placed on religious identity before attempting to market in religious social networks.

The increasing use of the Internet and social media as a result of glo-balization provides businesses with a new avenue for specifically targeting religious groups.[42] For example, there are now Facebook pages specifi-cally for Muslims in America, Baptists in Orlando, or Taoists in Canada, in addition to Facebook groups for specific churches, synagogues, and mosques in cities around the world. Additionally, this age of Big Data provides key insights into consumer religious profiles. This data can then be used to develop target segments, design new product offerings, and adjust advertising campaigns based on the desires associated with the religions most represented in the target segments.

An interesting distinction can be made between religion online (just information about religious topics) and online religion (interaction, discussion, actual online services, etc.).[43] Interactive online religion sites provide businesses with numerous opportunities to engage with religious consumers who have self-identified with religious social groups. Whether it is online religion sites, social media pages for religious groups, or in-person religious networks, each of these groups provide a consumer the opportunity to build and express his or her identity. Because identity is involved, these religious social groups have a great ability to influence purchase decisions and other consumer behaviors. Businesses should be pro-active in understanding the religious identity of the company's target market to better develop product and service offerings that the consumer wants and that match the consumer's identity.

Psychology Theory and Religious Behavior

Psychologists have proposed several theories to account for human behavior in response to religion, which, of course, also have implications for the specialized subtopic of consumer behavior.[44] Jaynes claims that humans have developed religion to externalize hallucinations that function to promote social control and human survival.[45] "God" is a hallucinated voice that directs people to behave in ways consistent with their survival, in his view. An alternative evolutionary theory from Boyer starts by recognizing the importance of cognition in systematizing folk wisdom, reproduction success, and survival strategies.[46] Brains have evolved to accommodate religion because religion enhances reproduction and survival.

Psychoanalytic theories often also point to the sexual importance of religion. Freud related religion to psycho-sexual conflict. Jung took a more positive approach to religion, viewing it as a repository of the collective unconscious, providing symbolic archetypes to transmit social wisdom.

Alfred Adler emphasized more cognitive goals and motives.[47] He saw religion as a way of dealing with human inferiorities by developing an ideal of the perfect (God) that animates human striving. Erickson sees religion as a mechanism that promotes growth through stages of development.[48] People develop identities via religion and other means that help them internalize cultural virtues. Fromm's *Psychoanalysis and Religion* presented perhaps the most sophisticated psychoanalytic approach to religion, suggesting that religion perpetuates the childish desire for a strong parental authority and protecting figure.[49] Religion can promote healthy mental functioning but can also lead to neuroses. In general psychoanalytic approaches have declined in influence among contemporary psychology researchers.

More cognitive theories have predominated in recent years. William James started much of the conversation in this area with his book *Varieties of Religious Experience*.[50] He distinguished sharply between institutional religion and personal religion, which today we might call organized religion versus spirituality. He had a much greater respect for and interest in spirituality, especially as experienced by the individual. His philosophy of pragmatism implies that religious practices that work for an individual will persist and that ones with little efficacy will wither.

Earlier we introduced Allport's notion of intrinsic versus extrinsic religion.[51] Intrinsic religion is more authentic and open, whereas extrinsic religion is more driven by superficial stereotypes. Allport developed measures for testing his hypotheses about religion. In part because of his commitment to empiricism, his theories have been influential.

Pargament described a theory of four approaches to religion: *rejectionist, exclusivist, constructivist,* and *pluralist* stances.[52] These approaches affect the relation between religion and coping behaviors, and they are especially important in psychotherapy. He uses the language of means-ends and adaptation, which are quite compatible to our perspective. The relationship with God can be significant for a client in coping with the stresses of life.

Humanistic psychologists emphasize the link between religion and values in adapting to life situations. Frankl described his survival in a Nazi concentration camp as centered on his religious and most important values.[53] He coined the term "Sunday neurosis" to describe the sense of emptiness, apathy, and boredom people feel once their work-week ends and they ponder the existential meaninglessness of their lives. Religion can provide a means to overcome that emptiness and move beyond the sense of the absurdity of existence.

If Frankl emphasized the lowest of the low (concentration camps) in developing his theory of religion, Maslow emphasized the highest of the high. He focused on peak experiences in his discussion of religion, which he described as "the private, lonely, personal illumination, revelation, or ecstasy of some acutely sensitive prophet or seer."[54] All high religion relates to peak experiences, which help people find existential meaning and transform their lives. Although we do not agree with all of Maslow's theories about the hierarchical nature of values, this perspective warrants further study.

An interesting more recent development is the application of attribution theory to the study of religion and consumer behavior.[55] How people explain phenomena influences how they respond to things.[56] Interjecting religious explanations into an understanding of the world changes how one responds to events.

All of these theories have at least some empirical support, but none have status as paradigmatic approaches to the topic. A good theory not only needs to explain the purpose of religion in a psychological context but also to explain the numerous empirical benefits of religion, such as highly religious individuals being much healthier than less or non-religious individuals.[57] As Hood and colleagues state, "Within the psychology of religion, the cry for good theory remains at the level of cacophony."[58] Since the ultimate goal of science is to develop theory, we hope that these theories will motivate further explanation and application in the area of religion and consumer behavior.

CHAPTER 8

Managerial Implications for Businesses

Although implications for businesses have been discussed throughout this book, this chapter is devoted to recapping these previous recommendations along with providing a course of action for businesses. The key takeaway point is that religion influences consumer behavior. Businesses need to step away from exclusive reliance on traditional demographic (e.g., age, gender, education) and psychographic (e.g., personality, lifestyle) descriptors of a target market and examine how religion defines the core values of the target market. We are not advocating ignoring other demographic and psychographic influencers but rather proposing to include religion in the mix. Effective marketing must realize the importance of understanding core values that then lead to attitudes and beliefs and ultimately purchase behavior. Table 8.1 provides a summary of key takeaways for businesses.

Why Should We Care That Religion Be Studied More in Behavioral Economics?

Increased globalization has created new means for marketing religious or spiritual goods as well as targeting people who are religious.[2] Sophisticated research techniques are available to help us better understand the core demographics and psychographics of a target market. Globalization has allowed these target markets to expand beyond the bounds of one locality. Thus, it is now possible that a religious product targeted toward Taoists can be marketed to Taoist communities around the world rather than just in Taoist-predominant communities (e.g., Taiwan). Also, international marketers have the opportunity to target advertising to specific religious groups based on the wants and needs of the religious group.

Table 8.1. Key Takeaways for Businesses on the Influence of Religion on Behavioral Economics

Why should we care?
Increase in globalization creates new means for targeting religious consumers.
Social media allow news to spread fast, need to be alert to cultural customs.
Religion is equally important, if not more important, for international advertisers to understand.
Religious affiliation is a viable basis for market segmentation.
Five tips for success are: (1) know your customers, (2) recognize adherence/religiosity level, (3) be conscious of limited consumer time, (4) address religious community, (5) be ready for change.[1]
In advertising
Religious individuals are more likely to view gender/sex related products as controversial.
Timing of controversial ads should be considered (e.g., after children's bedtimes).
Muslims want more advertising regulation, Christians and Hindus feel current regulation is good, Buddhists and Taoists want less regulation.
Religious consumers seek word-of-mouth recommendations from religious in-group.
In new product development
Examine target market's religion and religiosity before prototype is developed.
Takeoff time for new work-related products in highly religious countries is slower in comparison to less religious countries.
Catholics perceive more risk in purchase decisions than Jews and thus advertising may need to address risk concerns.
In market strategy
Religion is a necessity in determining overall market strategy.
Ignoring religion can result in offending a consumer's core values, failing to create targeted advertisements, and potentially miss an entire market opportunity.
Religious targeted products (e.g., *halal* or *kosher*) foods are purchased by non-religious consumers as well.
Religion helps to provide a more detailed understanding of target market wants and needs.
In business interactions
Highly religious employees lay greater emphasis on moral behavior and are more likely to see behaviors as controversial.
Allowing freedom to wear religious clothing (e.g., the Muslim's *hijab*) is important to religious individuals feeling a sense of connection to a business.
Frontline employees need to be trained in consumer's religious customs so as to not offend consumers during personal interactions.
Business marketers need to be aware of client's religious values to create advertisements and offer products in conjunction with the client's values.

A clear understanding of religious differences is important for businesses, especially ones involved in advertising[3] and branding.[4] Businesses involved in advertising and branding should become intimately aware of what is perceived as distasteful and immoral among religious groups in the company's target market. Especially for international businesses, it is important to realize that many advertisements cannot be standardized across countries.[5] For example, a risqué advertisement of a woman in a bikini in America would not be acceptable in the predominantly Muslim country of Saudi Arabia. On the other hand, it might not even be viewed as risqué in secular communities in France. With reference to this example, businesses need to be especially aware of customs and national laws regarding portrayal of women in advertisements.[6] Many times, advertisements are only as culturally sensitive as the designer is aware of the target market's religious customs.[7] With the advent of social media, animosity toward a company can be spread across the world in a matter of seconds after a consumer sees an advertisement that goes against his or her religious beliefs and norms.

For example, it is essential for international businesses to understand Muslim *fatwas* (prohibitions against certain products, services, or behaviors).[8] However, these *fatwas* may be hard to find with some *fatwas* listed in religious materials, whereas others are portrayed in the mass media.[9] Understanding *fatwas* can be more complicated than it seems, as in Malaysia alone there are 14 different *fatwa* committees.[10] However, in countries with a smaller Muslim presence, the national *fatwa* committee may be easier to identify. For example, in the United States, the Assembly of Muslim Jurists in America (AMJA) contains the *Fatwa* Committee and the *Fatwa* Advisory Board. The AMJA would be a first stop for businesses wanting to target Muslims in America to learn about the latest *fatwas*.

In addition, there are 12 main *fatwa* categories: fundamental beliefs, Islamic tax, religious rituals and practices, marriage issues, economic issues, medical issues, food and beverages, apparel, animals, social/Islamic law, *Muamalah*, and others—all of which international businesses should be aware of to avoid the risk of offending a Muslim consumer.[11] Additionally, commercials and other product promotions are not allowed during the five Muslim prayer times of the day that last 10–20 minutes per prayer session, for example in Muslim-predominant country of Saudi Arabia.[12]

A study assessing attitudes toward the introduction of television advertising in Saudi Arabia found a significant group of consumers who opposed television commercials because of a strong focus on western culture.[13] In this case, businesses in Saudi Arabia, or any international business, need to adjust advertisements to the local culture. Adjustments require careful introduction and consultation with religious locals. For example, the introduction of Mecca Cola attempted to address religious hesitations against Coca Cola but failed to fully address the reasons Muslims were opposed to buying Coca Cola in the first place.[14] Muslim consumers thought that by holding a mirror to the Coca Cola trademark, a slanderous message against Muslims appeared. As a result, Mecca Cola failed miserably.

Understanding the religious beliefs of customers does not dictate corporate transformation. Many multinational corporations such as Nestle, McDonalds, and L'Oreal have incorporated *halal* (permissible to Muslims) or Kosher (Jewish acceptable) product lines into their offerings.[15] Thus, the companies offer goods that are targeted toward religious groups and other goods that are not. Incorporating a consumer's religious affiliation could take only minor adjustments (e.g., offer an additional product variety, change the text in an advertisement). Many religious specialty markets are also increasing as consumers hold to religious standards to seek religious identity, such as how Muslims in America and other countries have increased *halal* sensitivity as Muslim consumers hold more strongly to the Muslim religious identity in surrounding multinational environments.[16]

Alserhan contends that adjusting product lines for different religious affiliations and associated laws increases brand loyalty.[17] Companies should realize that having a product offering adhering to a certain religion's beliefs does not limit sales of that product only to those religious adherents.[18] In fact, the majority of consumers of Kosher products are not actually Jewish but rather Muslims, vegetarians, and others.[19]

Heiman and colleagues provide five tips for businesses with regards to religious beliefs: (1) know your customers, (2) recognize the adherence/religiosity level (i.e., are religious prohibitions followed?), (3) be conscious of limited customer time, (4) market to/address the religious community, not just the individual, and (5) be ready for change![20] Following these five steps can help businesses to incorporate religion into a more holistic understanding of the company's target market and better develop product and service offerings that are targeted toward the consumer's wants and needs.

Religious affiliation is a viable basis for market segmentation[21] for academics and practitioners alike.[22] In addition, religion is a potential niche market for many goods and services.[23] Especially because religion and religiosity are easily observable constructs, businesses should take advantage of the insight that consumers' religious affiliation and religiosity offers companies.[24] For example, when studies find a particular religion or denomination to be more active in participating in a particular service industry, companies should utilize this knowledge and target service advertisements to the desiring religion or denomination.[25]

In Advertising

Research examining religion's influence on marketing communications is very limited.[26] Results from one of the few studies assessing religion and advertising mediums show that highly religious consumers are less apt to read the newspaper yet more likely to read certain magazines (e.g., Guideposts) and listen to Christian radio or television programming. These communication preferences for religious consumers provide businesses with a basis for understanding how to market to the religious segment.[27] However, much more research needs to be conducted in this area including assessing differences between religious affiliations.

Differences between less religious and more religious consumers extend into views of advertisements as well. Highly religious individuals of all religious affiliations view gender/sex related products and addictive products as more controversial in advertisements than those people who are less religious.[28] Thus, businesses selling these types of products should proceed cautiously in advertising to highly religious communities (e.g., the southeast Bible Belt of America). Also, the advertising medium and timing of advertising for these products should be chosen wisely. For example, if desiring to advertise contraception on television, it would be wise to limit advertising to late night when kids are most likely asleep and perhaps to avoid certain shows that are highly moral or family-oriented. In addition, conservative Muslims who are highly religious have significantly more negative attitudes toward advertisements as well as lower recall and unaided recall of both contentious and non-contentious advertisements in comparison to less religious Muslims.[29]

In comparing religious affiliations, Muslims are more likely to see advertising regulations as not stringent enough, Christians and Hindus feel that regulations are currently acceptable, and Buddhists and Taoists feel like current advertising regulations are too stringent.[30] These advertising regulations apply to many types of products including controversial products (e.g., alcohol or cigarettes), controversial narratives (e.g., violence), or controversial content (e.g., nudity). These negative perceptions of advertising could be due to highly religious consumers viewing advertising in general as a deceptive and persuasive practice.

Religion also influences where consumers go to seek information about products. Highly religious consumers prefer word of mouth recommendations from a religious in-group and look less to their significant other or external information sources (e.g., television, Internet, magazines).[31] This is in accordance with the previous chapter's discussion on the influence of religious social groups on consumer behavior. Thus, understanding word of mouth within a religious social network is more important to a business than designing targeted advertisements.

In New Product Development

Just as with any product, businesses involved with new product development should understand the product's target market and the associated religious affiliation and religiosity level. This understanding of the product's target market should be achieved at the market research stage rather than waiting until after a prototype has been developed or the product is in full distribution.

In general, nations with overall higher religiosity have slightly slower takeoff times for new work-related products compared to less religious countries.[32] Fun products show no difference in takeoff time between highly religious and less religious countries. The slower takeoff for work-related products could be because of higher levels of perceived risk with the work-related product not working properly. In Chapter 7 discussing religion and risky behavior, the results of a research study were discussed that showed that Catholics perceive more risk in purchase decisions than Jews. Thus, predominantly Catholic areas can be expected to have slower takeoff times for new products. Businesses desiring to increase takeoff times should employ measures to decrease risk perceptions (e.g., offer a money back guarantee or a warranty).

In Market Strategy

Any marketing plan should include discussion of the pertinent religious factors. By this point in the book, it should be clear that both religious affiliation and religiosity significantly influence consumer behavior. A business would be foolish to ignore religion completely. Ignoring religion can offend a consumer's religious values, fail to create advertisements that address the needs and concerns of religious consumers, and also miss an entire market for a current product offering or miss an opportunity for a profitable new product line. International marketing strategy should pay particularly close attention to religious values and incorporate these into how marketing strategy is adapted to each country.

Businesses could benefit from integrating niche religious target markets into an overall marketing strategy. For example, a food manufacturer could develop a niche target market offering *halal* or *kosher* foods that attract new business from Muslims and Jews, respectively. As mentioned previously, offering products that are targeted at specific religious groups does not limit sales to only consumers from these religious affiliations. Many health-conscious consumers or consumers with allergies to certain food products also prefer to buy food products that contain *halal* or *kosher* labels. Niche target markets directed toward religious consumers are just one way among many to integrate religion into a company's overall market strategy. Whether it is through niche target markets, adapting advertising to religious values, or researching the religiosity level of a product's current target market, religion should be a key consumer characteristic that businesses examine.

In Business Interactions

This book is focused on how religious belief systems influence consumer behavior, and ultimately behavioral economics. However, it is worth mentioning that religion influences many other aspects of business as well, including how employees interact with one another. Highly religious employees exhibit the same behaviors as mentioned throughout this book, such as a greater emphasis on moral behavior, seeing more products and behaviors as controversial, and also wearing religious garments (e.g., the *burqa* for Muslims). An understanding of the faith of other employees within an organization can help to avoid offending other employees and to create a more cohesive, collegial business unit. These observations are especially important in service organizations where employees *are* a major part of the "product." The same principles, of course, apply to interactions between a sales person and a customer. Sometimes sensitivity to religion requires actively avoiding the invoking of religion.

Outside of an organization, many business marketers are involved in discussions with clients of other religious affiliations, especially with international clients. A marketer would be wise to understand the client's religious affiliation in order to create advertisements that do not offend a client's wants, needs, and products. Even if an advertisement is appropriate for the target market of a client's product, a controversial advertisement could be perceived as offensive if the client is highly religious. Thus, marketers should use the knowledge of how religion influences consumer behavior and be sensitive to relationships with clients and internal employees as well.

CHAPTER 9

Cases

This chapter explores the influence of religion on consumer behavior through a series of three case studies. The first case study examines Best Buy's controversial advertising practice in 2009 when the company provided greetings for a Muslim holiday in a weekly circular advertisement during the traditional American holiday season. The second case study investigates how religion and politics are tightly intertwined and the challenges businesses need to address as the Hispanic population and associated religious values continue to increase in America. Finally, the third case examines pro-social advertising with sustainable marketing and investigates how religious affiliation influences adoption of sustainable consumption practices.

Best Buy and Holiday Advertising

In 2009, Best Buy distributed its annual Black Friday sales ad in thousands of newspapers across the United States, but this time with a twist: in a small bubble at the bottom of the page were the words "Happy Eid al-Adha," recognizing a Muslim holiday.[1] Consumer groups criticized this ad and argued that supporting the Muslim holiday was an anti-American action that took away from the Thanksgiving celebration. As one consumer states:

"I am boycotting Best Buy and will shop online instead from now on! I am an atheist, but avoiding the use of such words, such as Merry Christmas, in a country that was founded on these principles and whose population is primarily Christian is insulting even to me! I mean where does it end? This is America, and I as an immigrant myself, adapted to its culture and customs, and I never tried to impose those of my native country which I grew up with! IF other people do not like this country's culture, customs, and traditions, then LEAVE!!!"

In contrast, some consumers supported Best Buy and thanked the company for acknowledging Muslims in America. Muslims represent only 0.6%

of the American population, which makes Muslims a niche target market. Although there is an American Muslim Consumer Conference each year, very little targeted marketing toward Muslims occurs in the United States, especially among larger Fortune 500 companies.[2] Just as Muslims are a minority in the United States, supportive comments toward Best Buy's advertisement were also a minority in relation to the plethora of negative remarks. Positive remarks reflected Best Buy's openness. For example:

"Good for Best Buy! We live in a country that is supposed to be inclusive of all religions, not just Christian."

"I applaud Best Buy for wanting to create a brand that is well suited to any American community in which they have a store."

"I am happy Best Buy is making an effort to reach out to Muslims. Muslims are a minority religion here, and one could argue that the majority (Christians) do not need an extra effort made to make them feel welcome (even by a retailer) because, well, they're the majority."

"Thank you Best Buy for the Eid Greetings!! I plan to spend more money at Best Buy. Thank you for being inclusive of various cultures."

Best Buy is not just any small consumer store. Best Buy is the world's largest consumer electronics store, so making a move toward targeting a religious niche has the potential to greatly influence future religious niche marketing. Best Buy's consumer base has been growing ever since its inception in 1966. Today, Best Buy receives over one million visitors to BestBuy.com and over 600 million visitors to Best Buy physical stores each year. Annual revenues for Best Buy exceed $50 billion across its 1,400 physical store locations.[3]

When Best Buy created an advertisement acknowledging the Muslim holiday of Eid al-Adha, Best Buy honored one of Islam's major religious festivals. Eid al-Adha, also known as Feast of the Sacrifice, is a day of celebration when the prophet Abraham was called by God to sacrifice his firstborn son. Abraham followed God's call, and God then saved Abraham's firstborn son by providing a lamb instead to be sacrificed. Sacrifice is a common basis of many Western religions where a sacrifice is offered to account for human sin. Abraham is one of the few people in Western religious doctrine who followed the calling of God, and therefore Abraham and this occasion are celebrated as a time of reverence to God. For Muslims, Eid is a time of prayer and religious services, and, in some areas, animal sacrifice. The background story of the festival (i.e., Abraham following God's commandments) is found in all Western religions, but the actual festival is only celebrated by Muslims. However, most consumers, including Christians, hearing about Eid al-Adha for the first time in the Best Buy ad, were not aware of this similarity.

Best Buy's response to the ensuing controversy was: "We do use the word 'holiday' in some of our advertising because it is meant to be inclusive to everyone. However, just as we have in the past, we will also reference specific holidays such as Christmas, Hanukkah, and Kwanzaa in our weekly ads, store signage and other advertising vehicles."[4]

In spite of comments on either side of the religious debate (either target Muslims or target only Christians), one segment of consumers would prefer no mention of religion at all. This segment of consumers sees a separation between business and religious practices. For example:

"Who except atheists and religious fanatics cares which religious days BestBuy mentions? I go to BestBuy to buy gadgets, not to see if they respect my religious beliefs so grow up."

Is it really possible to separate business and religion? Would a company be seen as aloof if it made no mention of any holiday during the holiday season? These questions are tough ones that Best Buy, and any business that advertises, must address.

In Best Buy's attempt to tap into a new market segment, the company likely did not expect the controversy that was to come. In spite of the numerous derogatory comments aimed at Best Buy, still a segment of consumers understood Best Buy's practices as a business strategy. This segment of consumers understood how business and religion are delicately intertwined. Religion is a defining element of a consumer's belief system, and therefore businesses should capitalize on this fact and design marketing campaigns to target consumers' core beliefs. For example:

"I am a Christian, but I don't mind that they mention the Muslim holiday. They just want to make some money. I would do it too if it guarantees me at least $1 million more in revenues."

"I guess Best Buy figures they'll get more business if they are more inclusive, which is a good strategy. Can't believe there are people who have problems with a company wishing Eid-al-Adha. Best Buy wished a Happy Easter holiday, so I don't understand what's the big deal considering Eid falls on black Friday."

"Yes—as shocking as it may seem—retailers are going to spend most of their time and effort going after the biggest pool of customers! Best Buy is not some type of equal opportunity program—they're a business looking to make money. Being inclusive, when it doesn't cost extra, is the most you can expect—not for them to create flyers and sales and signage for everyone's favorite holidays."

However, if consumers perceived Best Buy's approach as purely business and done in a cynical effort to seek more profit, is it worth the added pressure and demands placed on the public relations department at Best Buy? As one consumer states it:

"While I applaud and support Best Buy and other retailers who become inclusive in their approach to retailing, their motivation remains economic rather ecumenical."

What is Best Buy to do? Consumers are voicing strong opinions in Best Buy forums, on various news sites, in personal blogs, and across numerous private discussion forums. A simple statement that was made to target a new religious market has turned into a public relations nightmare.

It is not only Best Buy that faces criticism about religious-oriented advertising. Hallmark features cards for Muslim holidays, and Ann Taylor, ESPN, and Verizon have created Muslim-targeted portions of their websites. Each year around the holiday season, companies are faced with the decision of what to mention in advertising—"happy holidays," "Merry Christmas," "Happy Hanukkah," among others. Companies that provide no mention of the holidays can be seen as cold and aloof, but companies that make any mention to the holidays can be called out as favoring one religious group. What is a company to do?

Case Questions:

1. Was Best Buy's decision to target a religious minority a good idea? Why or why not?
2. What should Best Buy do now to handle the consumer backlash?
3. Should Best Buy target religious minorities in the future?
4. How should other companies that would like to tap into these unreached religious markets proceed?

Political Marketing and Religious Groups

In the United States, Catholics constitute roughly a quarter of the population; thus, as a political group Catholics are quite meaningful. Politicians, especially in heavily Catholic areas, need to attend to the issues and concerns of Catholics. Before Ronald Reagan, Catholics tended to vote mostly for Democrats because the Democratic Party showed more concern about helping the poor and downtrodden, concerns of traditional Catholic teachings. During the past generation, however, more conservative Catholics with strong views against abortion and gay rights have exerted increasing influence and contributed to more Republican votes from Catholics. Not only have these changes occurred, but spending on political marketing has also increased to the point where several billion dollars was spent on marketing for the 2012 presidential election.

One of the fastest-growing demographic groups in the United States, and therefore an important group to consider, is the Hispanic group. Hispanics are almost entirely Catholic, and their voting has trended heavily Democratic. George W. Bush, a former Governor of border-state Texas, did fairly well with Hispanic voters, perhaps because working well with Hispanics is a virtue in Texas politics. However, in the 2008 and 2012 presidential elections Hispanic voters heavily tilted toward the Democrats, although Republicans still carried Texas, as they have since 1976. Republican rhetoric, especially during the primary season, often advocated strict punishment of "illegal immigrants," and Hispanic voters perceived that a Republican administration would not be friendly toward them. As Catholics, Hispanic voters have sided with the anti-poverty position more than the anti-gay position, perhaps because they are more likely to experience personal consequences, such as poverty, related to economic issues.

Texas is especially fascinating because, although Republicans have dominated it in recent years, it has the potential to change because of the heavy influx of Hispanics. Over the past decade, 65% of the population growth in Texas has been Hispanic. One forecast is that by 2030, Hispanics will grow to 43% of the Texas population, versus a drop from 50% to 39% for the white population. Hispanics, however, have not tended to vote heavily. In 2012, Hispanics represented 38% of the population but only 22% of the voters. Stated another way, 2.2 million eligible Hispanics did not vote in Texas in 2012.[5] If half of these nonvoters had instead voted for Barack Obama, he would have carried Texas and its rich store of electoral votes.

Another trend is Hispanics leaving Catholic churches and instead joining Protestant churches, especially very conservative Protestant denominations.[6] One estimate is that by 2030, half of Hispanics in the United States will be Protestant, not Catholic. Some Hispanics see Catholicism as what they left behind in Latin America and Protestantism as the pathway to middle-class life in the United States. On issues of personal morality, these Protestant denominations that Hispanics are joining tend to advocate very conservative ideals, yet many denominations advocate for a greater role for women in the church and a much more progressive government policy on immigration.

Case questions:

1. If you were a Republican strategist in Texas, how would you respond religiously to the changing Hispanic population?
2. What if you were a Democratic strategist?
3. What if your job were to retain Hispanics within the Catholic faith? What would you do?

Religion and Sustainable Public Policy

Interest in sustainable products and green advertising is rapidly increasing. According to a recent study by Environmental Leader, 82% of companies plan to increase spending on green marketing.[7] From a consumer perspective, the spending power of consumers with sustainability and environmental concerns is more than $230 billion.[8] With such a large business and consumer market and a growing demand for sustainable public policy, an understanding of the consumer factors (e.g., core values) driving sustainable behaviors, and more specifically sustainable purchase behaviors, is needed.

Many studies have assessed the relationship among basic demographics and psychographics and sustainable purchase behaviors, but research has not adequately investigated the potential influence of core religious values on sustainable purchase and non-purchase related behaviors.[9] Would policy development and associated consumer acceptance of policies be improved if policies were adapted toward a consumer's core religious value system?

Take the case of sustainable energy, for example. Many new public policies are being developed to encourage the use of renewable energy over other forms of energy, such as diesel. Consumers whose value systems are developed out of Western religions might believe that there is a distinct end to this world in the future when the religious savior returns to bring all believers into heaven. In this view, consumers of Western religions may feel that renewable energy projects are a waste of money because the world will soon come to an end, resulting in no need for renewable energy. In fact, many religious consumers would prefer to hear about the financial saving benefits of sustainable products rather than the earth-saving benefits.

One of the earliest discussions on environmental behavior and religion goes back to the famous Lynn White thesis.[10] White's thesis analyzes Christian doctrine, specifically the book of Genesis in the Bible, identifying repetition of the doctrine stating human's control over nature (e.g., humans naming the animals, humans exploiting nature for their benefit) and purports that Christians are less environmentally-friendly as a result. White's thesis suggests that Christians who believe every word of the Bible to be true also believe that nature is to be used for the needs of humanity and that priority in everyday actions should be given to evangelizing rather than preserving the environment. Follow up studies confirm White's thesis linking inerrant belief in the Bible to less concern for the environment[11] and fewer sustainable consumption practices.[12]

However, more recent competing research shows that participation in sustainable behaviors is dependent upon personal factors, including values, with the more altruistic consumers more likely to participate in sustainable behaviors.[13] Additionally, values related to helping others lead to increased participation in sustainable behaviors.[14] Looking at the antecedents to altruism and values of helping, strong intrinsic religious beliefs have long been shown to be driving causes of altruism and helping behaviors.[15] Research also shows that religious values, in general, are a primary determinant of a consumer's core values,[16] and these core values relate directly to consumer attitudes and behaviors.[17]

Additionally, sustainability is being encouraged within the church, such as with the Genesis Covenant, which encourages churches to reduce their environmental footprint.[18] As a result, this competing research shows that highly religious consumers may be more likely to participate in sustainable behaviors when the need for the behavior is framed in an altruistic way (e.g., "help others by helping the environment") rather than just a way to preserve the planet (e.g., "help save the environment for generations to come").

For differences among specific religious affiliations, James asserts that Western religions (Christianity, Judaism, Islam) believe that God created nature and therefore God and humans hold a superior position to nature.[19] Eastern religions (Buddhism, Hinduism, Confucianism, Taoism), on the other hand, follow a pantheistic view that God is in and through everything, including nature. Sarre[20] expands on this distinction between Western and Eastern religions, arguing that Western religions follow White's thesis that God created nature, God gave control of nature to humans, and therefore Western religions should be less apt to be environmentally-friendly.[21] Eastern religious affiliations follow the pantheistic view that destroying an element of nature is destroying part of God or other divine being and, therefore, should be more likely to participate in environmentally-friendly efforts.[22]

Both the Western and Eastern religious views on environmental behaviors could lead to very different methods for promoting public policy. Although consumers adhering to Eastern religions may prefer advertisements such as "save nature, save God," consumers adhering to Western religions may instead prefer more of a directive statement, such as "God wants you to care for nature because He created it." Because sustainable consumption is a means by which to express environmentally-friendly attitudes and beliefs, consumers adhering to Eastern religious beliefs are expected to participate significantly more in sustainable purchase and non-purchase behaviors in comparison to consumers adhering to Western religious beliefs.

However, many religious consumers may prefer that public policies avoid targeting specific religious groups as the targeting effort is just seen as a marketing tactic. These religious consumers may feel that targeting sustainable policies towards specific religious groups is the same as politicians targeting groups in pre-election advertising; the advertising is purely a method for attracting support, and the creator of the advertisement has no care for the well-being of the religious group members. If consumers do not trust the sustainable policy makers, then producing advertising targeted at specific religious groups could actually make religious consumers less likely to support the sustainable policy than if no targeted marketing campaigns were developed in the first place.

Another issue that must be addressed if sustainable public policy is to be targeted toward specific religious groups is how to reach these religious consumers. Placing targeted advertisements in national newspapers may reach the target segment, but there will also be a large amount of waste exposure to consumers who are outside the target segment of religious consumers. Directing advertisements at religious organizations has the potential to be rejected by the organization as not wanting to accept marketed messages. Or, if the message is accepted, religious organizations may use the funds received from distributing the marketing message to contribute to the mission of the religious organization and to convey to organizations' members that the sustainable policy message is of little importance.

If a sustainable policy message is designed in a way that it is perceived as truthful and trustworthy, then distributing the message through a religious organization would be the most effective means of reaching the target market because there would be no waste exposure to consumers who are not religious. The Internet and social media provide new avenues for targeted advertising that those involved in sustainable policy development may find useful in the future for encouraging adoption of sustainable public policy.[23] As the need for sustainability becomes increasingly important and public policy makers face increased pressure to ensure policy adoption (and acceptance of related programs), targeting consumers' core religious values becomes an increasingly important opportunity to consider.

Case Questions:

1. Should policy makers tailor sustainable policy to the religious value systems of consumers? Why or why not?

2. In the case of policies to encourage development of renewable energy sources, what can policy makers do to target consumers adhering to Western vs. Eastern religions? How might addressing consumers' religious values help in acceptance of sustainable public policy? How could it hinder acceptance?

3. If sustainable policy is targeted at specific religious groups, what method(s) of advertising should be used to reach consumers? What distribution channels (e.g., internet, newspaper, church bulletins, religious magazines, social media) should be used to reach religious consumers?

CHAPTER 10

Conclusion

Recapping: Why Belief Systems?

Belief systems are composed of core values. Vast amounts of research show that core values are strongly linked with consumer behavior. Thus, an understanding of belief systems is critical for understanding consumer behavior. Belief systems can be dictated by culture, but more often than not are based on religious affiliation. Even cultural beliefs are influenced by religious beliefs.

Religious belief systems develop from religious doctrine and scriptures as well as from teachings of religious leaders. These religious beliefs influence everyday behavior, longevity of consumers, and dictate moral behavior, among other things. Thus, it is vital that businesses understand religious belief systems and associated levels of devotion to these belief systems (i.e., religiosity) to be most effective in marketing practices.

Businesses and behavioral economists have historically studied religion less than is warranted by its importance. One possible reason for this dearth of research is the sheer complexity of religion. We have seen that some studies fail to discover the influence of religion because they oversimplify the concepts and groups associated with religion or oversimplify the nature of the relations between religion and behavior. Religious perspectives are diverse and complex. There is a broad and ever-complicated array of denominations and religious perspectives, and simple-minded breakdowns are bound to miss subtle nuances. With the advent of Big Data access and analysis techniques, using this excuse to avoid the obvious influence of religion is less understandable.

Recapping: Managerial Implications

Businesses can greatly benefit from incorporating religion into marketing strategy and definition of target markets. Businesses can create niche

markets targeted toward specific religious affiliations and religiosity levels, such as a market for *halal* or *kosher* products. Also, by developing a
more comprehensive definition of target markets that includes religion,
businesses will know what products and advertisements would be offensive to consumers. For example, marketing skimpy clothing or ads with
women empowerment may be seen as offensive to Muslim consumers
but would be seen as more acceptable to progressive Christian denominations. Businesses desiring to target a certain religious group should conduct research to determine when and where the target market consumes
media (e.g., watching late night clean comedy on ABC) and can then
design advertisements to be broadcasted or distributed in these locations
and times.

In addition, many religious affiliations prohibit use of certain products, such as alcohol and drugs. Companies that are marketing products
in these product categories or developing advertising that incorporates
these elements can help prevent offending a large segment of religious
consumers by understanding religious prohibitions. In addition to better
understanding the target market of a company's products, an understanding of how religion influences consumer behavior will also assist businesses
in communication with people of other religious beliefs, including other
employees within the company and communication with external clients.
Religion has been around for thousands of years (or longer depending on
the religious faith tradition), and businesses need to finally take notice of
the influence religion has on every day behavior to create more effective
marketing campaigns that fulfill both the needs of the businesses and of
the consumer.

Given the importance and complexity of religion and belief systems,
as well as the technological progress of the recent past, the desirability
of direct targeting and direct marketing through such selective means as
social media and direct mail becomes ever more attractive. A mass media
purchase in a large market will almost inevitably reach both receptive
and non-receptive audiences. In today's multicultural environment, businesses need to use their resources efficiently and effectively.

In addition to direct marketing and social media, we are now in an
age of Big Data meaning that access to large databases with a vast amount
of consumer information is widely available. Obtaining information on

a market segment's religious affiliation and degree of religiosity is easier than ever before. Even if a company does not directly ask the consumer his or her religious affiliation, this information can be easily obtainable by reviewing purchase behavior associated with a store loyalty card. If a consumer is seen purchasing Christian-related products, the consumer can be assumed to at least have some appreciation for the Christian faith. Similarly, if a consumer is seen purchasing Hindu products, the consumer can be assumed to have at least some appreciation for the Hindu faith. This data can then be used to create targeted advertisements and promotions to meet these consumers' religious needs as well as avoid offending the consumers with controversial advertising.

Big Data provide big information. Big information means that religious data are now more easily accessible than before. Because religion is at the core of consumer values and influences both religious and non-religious consumers alike, now is the time to act on Big Data through means such as direct marketing and social media to create better targeted products, more well-crafted and religiously-appropriate advertising, and redesigned marketing strategies to target consumers' core wants and needs. Clearly, religion and behavioral economics represent a duo that any business of today needs to understand, appreciate, and respect.

Appendix

Resources for Businesses on Religious Distributions

The following list of resources should help businesses desiring to understand the demographic breakdown of a geographic area with regards to religious affiliation. Note, however, that these general statistics may not apply to a business' target market; hence, further research is necessary to fully understand the religious affiliation and degree of religiosity of specific market segments.

Recent Research

- Association of Religious Data Archives: www.thearda.com
- Pew Forum for Religious Research: www.religions. pewforum.com
- Gallup, www.gallup.com/tag/religion.aspx
- American Attitudes: Who Thinks What about the Issues that Shape Our Lives, by New Strategist Publications (2010) – specific discussion on religious attitudes in America

Reference Books

- The Baker Pocket Guide to World Religions by Gerald McDermott (2008)
- AMG's Handi-Reference: World Religion's and Cults by John Hunt and Dan Penwell (2008)
- The World's Religions by Huston Smith (1991)

Notes

Chapter 1

1. Kahle and Valette (2012).
2. Sullivan (2009).
3. Evans and Berman (2010).
4. New Strategist Publications (2010).
5. New Strategist Publications (2010).
6. New Strategist Publications (2010).
7. New Strategist Publications (2010).
8. New Strategist Publications (2010).
9. Pew Forum on Religion and Public Life (2008).
10. Pew Forum on Religion and Public Life (2008).
11. National Retail Foundation (2012).
12. Nicolaievsky and Maenchen (1976).
13. Sherif (1935).
14. Stabile (2007).

Chapter 2

1. Reynolds and Olson (2001).
2. Pargament (2001)
3. Kahle (1983); Kahle, Beatty, and Homer (1986); Kahle (1996); Kahle, Rose, and Shoham (2000); Kahle and Valette (2012).
4. Merriam-Webster (2013).
5. Johnstone-Louis (2013).
6. Hood, Hill, and Spilka (2009).
7. Wilkes, Burnett, and Howell (1986), pp. 47–56.
8. Hood, Hill, and Spilka (2009).
9. Delener (1990), pp. 27–38.
10. Himmelfarb (1975), pp. 606–618.
11. Wilkes, Burnett, and Howell (1986), pp. 47–56.
12. Allport and Ross (1967), 432–443.
13. Hill et al. (2000), pp. 51–77.
14. Lenski (1963).
15. Kale (2004), pp. 92–107.
16. Hood, Hill, and Spilka (2009); Kale (2004), pp. 92–107; Zinnbauer (1997), pp. 549–564.

17. Emmons and Paloutzian (2003), pp. 377–402; Hill et al. (2000), pp. 51–77; Hood, Hill, and Spilka (2009); Zinnbauer (1997), pp. 549–564.

18. Hill et al. (2000), pp. 51–77.

19. Kale (2004), pp. 92–107.

20. Hill et al. (2000), pp. 51–77.

21. Taylor (2007).

22. Bowker (2006).

23. Essoo and Dibb (2004), pp. 683–712.

24. Faulkner and Dejong (1966), pp. 246–254; Hill et al. (2000), pp. 51–77; Himmelfarb (1975); King (1967); King and Hunt (1969), pp. 321–323; King and Hunt (1972), pp. 240–251; King and Hunt (1990), pp. 531–535; Lindridge (2005), pp. 142–151; McDaniel and Burnett (1990), pp. 101–112; Muhamad and Mizerski (2010), pp. 124–135; Wilkes, Burnett, and Howell (1986), pp. 47–56.

25. Hill et al. (2000), pp. 51–77.

26. Piedmont (1999), pp. 985–1013; Rican and Janosova (2010), pp. 2–13.

27. Seidlitz et al. (2002), pp. 439–453.

28. Dejong, Faulkner, and Warland (1976), pp. 866–889.

29. Wilkes, Burnett, and Howell (1986), pp. 47–56.

30. Wilkes, Burnett, and Howell (1986), pp. 47–56.

31. Himmelfarb (1975), pp. 606–618.

32. Himmelfarb (1975), pp. 606–618.

33. Dejong, Faulkner, and Warland (1976), pp. 866–889.

34. Faulkner and Dejong (1966), pp. 246–254.

35. King and Hunt (1969), pp. 321–323.

36. King (1967), pp. 173–190.

37. King and Hunt (1972), pp. 240–251; King and Hunt (1990), pp. 531–535.

38. Himmelfarb (1975), pp. 606–618.

39. McDaniel and Burnett (1990), pp. 101–112.

40. Hill and Hood (1999).

41. Wilkes, Burnett, and Howell (1986), pp. 47–56.

42. Allport and Ross (1967), pp. 432–443.

43. Allport and Ross (1967), pp. 432–443.

44. Choi, Kale, and Shin (2010), pp. 61–68; Delener (1990), pp. 27–38; Delener (1994), pp. 36–53; Essoo and Dibb (2004), pp. 683–712; Jianfeng, Hongping, and Lanying (2009), pp. 31–34; Wiebe and Fleck (1980), pp. 181–187.

45. Allport and Ross (1967), pp. 432–443.

46. Allport and Ross (1967), pp. 432–443.

47. Allport and Ross (1967), pp. 432–443.

48. Donahue (1985), pp. 418–423.

49. Donahue (1985), pp. 418–423.
50. Khraim (2010), pp. 166–179.
51. Cohen, Siegel, and Rozin (2003), pp. 287–295.
52. Khraim (2010), pp. 166–179.
53. Wilde and Joseph (1997), pp. 899–900.
54. Muhamad and Mizerski (2007), pp. 74–85.
55. Muhamad and Mizerski (2010), pp. 124–135.
56. Muhamad and Mizerski (2010), pp. 124–135.
57. Allport and Ross (1967), pp. 432–443.
58. Himmelfarb (1975), pp. 606–618.
59. Muhamad and Mizerski (2010), pp. 124–135.
60. Allport and Ross (1967), pp. 432–443.
61. Smidt et al. (2003), pp. 515–532.
62. Greeley (1963), pp. 21–31; Hirschman (1982), pp. 228–233.
63. Hirschman (1981), pp. 102–110; Hirschman (1983), pp. 131–170; McDaniel and Burnett (1990), pp. 101–112.
64. Engel (1976), pp. 98–101.
65. Babakus, Cornwell, Mitchell, and Schlegelmilch (2004), pp. 254–263.
66. Essoo and Dibb (2004), pp. 683–712.
67. Bailey and Sood (1993), pp. 328–352.
68. Heiman, Just, McWilliams, and Zilberman (2004), pp. 9–11.
69. Michell and Al-Mossawi (1999), pp. 427–444.
70. Smith (1990), pp. 225–245.
71. Forthun, Bell, Peek, and Sun (1999), pp. 75–90; Hoffmann and Miller (1998), pp. 528–546; Woodrum and Wolkomir (1997), pp. 223–234; Gay and Lynxwiler (2010), pp. 110–127; Wolkomir, Futreal, Woodrum, and Hoban (1997), pp. 325–343.
72. Hill and Hood (1999).
73. Bailey and Sood (1993), pp. 328–352.
74. Bailey and Sood (1993), pp. 328–352.
75. Bailey and Sood (1993), pp. 328–352.
76. Poria, Butler, and Airey (2003), pp. 340–363.
77. Babakus, Cornwell, Mitchell, and Schlegelmilch (2004), pp. 254–263; Cornwell et al. (2005), pp. 531–546; LaBarbera and Gurhan (1997), pp. 71–97; Oguinn and Belk (1989), pp. 227–238; Poria, Butler, and Airey (2003), pp. 340–363; Rindfleisch, Burroughs, and Wong (2005), pp. 153–154; Swinyard, Kau, and Phua (2001), pp. 13–32; Thompson and Raine (1976), pp. 71–78; Rindfleisch, Wong, and Burroughs (2010).
78. Haley, White, and Cunningham (2001); King (1967), pp. 173–190; LaBarbera and Gurhan (1997), pp. 71–97; Muhamad and Mizerski (2007), pp. 4–85; Sood and Nasu (1995), pp. 1–9; Bailey and Sood (1993), pp. 328–352.

79. Kahle, Kau, Tambyah, Tan, and Jung (2005); Ong and Moschis (2006), pp. 1–13.
80. Siguaw and Simpson (1997), pp. 23–40.
81. Delener (1990), pp. 27–38; Delener (1994), pp. 36–53; Doran and Natale (2011), pp. 1–15.
82. Essoo and Dibb (2004), pp. 683–712; Heiman, Just, McWilliams and Zilberman (2004), pp. 9–11; Hirschman (1982), pp. 228–233; McDaniel and Burnett (1990), pp. 101–112; McDaniel and Burnett (1991), pp. 26–33; Swinyard, Kau, and Phua (2001), pp. 13–32; Vitell and Paolillo (2003), pp. 151–162; Rindfleisch, Wong, and Burroughs (2010).
83. Chandrasekaran and Tellis (2008), pp. 844–860; Gross and Simmons (2009), pp. 101–129.
84. Cohen, Siegel and Rozin (2003), pp. 287–295.
85. Clark and Dawson (1996), pp. 359–372; Dotson and Hyatt (2000), pp. 63–68; Fam, Waller, and Erdogan (2004), pp. 537–555; Faulkner and Dejong (1966), pp. 246–254; Hirschman (1981), pp. 102–110; Mattila, Apostolopoulos, Sonmez, Yu, and Sasidharan (2001), p. 193; Michell and Al-Mossawi (1999), pp. 427–444; Muhamad and Mizerski (2007), pp. 74–85; Poulson, Eppler, Satterwhite, Wuensch, and Bass (1998), pp. 227–232; Rican and Janosova (2010), pp. 2–13; Taylor, Halstead, and Haynes (2010), pp. 79–92; Wiebe and Fleck (1980), pp. 181–187; Hashim and Mizerski (2010), pp. 37–50; Doran and Natale (2011), pp. 1–15; Swimberghe, Sharma, and Flurry (2009), pp. 340–347; Henley Jr, Philhours, Ranganathan, and Bush (2009), pp. 89–103.

Chapter 3

1. James (1902/2004).
2. Hofstede (1994), pp. 4–13; Hunt and Penwell (2008).
3. Hofstede (1994), pp. 4–13; Hunt and Penwell (2008).
4. James (1902/2004).
5. Hunt and Penwell (2008).
6. Rhodes (2005).
7. Bowker (2005).
8. Rhodes (2005).
9. Bailey and Sood (1993), pp. 328–352.
10. Rhodes (2005).
11. Rhodes (2005).
12. New Strategist Publications (2010).
13. Pew Forum on Religion and Public Life (2008).
14. Pew Forum on Religion and Public Life (2008).
15. Hunt and Penwell (2008).

16. Rhodes (2005).
17. Rhodes (2005).
18. Rhodes (2005).
19. Rhodes (2005).
20. New Strategist Publications (2010).
21. Pew Forum on Religion and Public Life (2008).
22. Bowker (2005); Hunt and Penwell (2008).
23. Rhodes (2005).
24. Atwood (2010).
25. Pew Forum on Religion and Public Life (2008).
26. Bowker (2005).
27. Hunt and Penwell (2008).
28. Rhodes (2005).
29. Rhodes (2005).
30. Pew Forum on Religion and Public Life (2008).
31. Bowker (2005).
32. Hunt and Penwell (2008).
33. Rhodes (2005).
34. Rhodes (2005).
35. Rhodes (2005).
36. Rhodes (2005).
37. Rhodes (2005).
38. Pew Forum on Religion and Public Life (2008).
39. Hunt and Penwell (2008).
40. Bowker (2005).
41. Rhodes (2005).
42. Rhodes (2005).
43. Rhodes (2005).
44. Rhodes (2005).
45. Rhodes (2005).
46. Pew Forum on Religion and Public Life (2008).
47. Pew Forum on Religion and Public Life (2008).
48. Bowker (2005).
49. Hunt and Penwell (2008).
50. Rhodes (2005).
51. Rhodes (2005).
52. Bowker (2005).
53. Rhodes (2005).
54. Rhodes (2005).
55. Pew Forum on Religion and Public Life (2008).
56. Hunt and Penwell (2008).
57. Rhodes (2005).

58. Bowker (2005).
59. Rhodes (2005).
60. Rhodes (2005).
61. Rhodes (2005).
62. Rhodes (2005).
63. Pew Forum on Religion and Public Life (2008).
64. Hunt and Penwell (2008).
65. Rhodes (2005).
66. Rhodes (2005).
67. Rhodes (2005).
68. Rhodes (2005).
69. Pew Forum on Religion and Public Life (2008).
70. Hunt and Penwell (2008).
71. Rhodes (2005).
72. Rhodes (2005).
73. Rhodes (2005).
74. Rhodes (2005).
75. Pew Forum on Religion and Public Life (2008).
76. Rhodes (2005).
77. Rhodes (2005).
78. Rhodes (2005).
79. Rhodes (2005).
80. Rhodes (2005).
81. Rhodes (2005).
82. Pew Forum on Religion and Public Life (2008).
83. Rhodes (2005).
84. Rhodes (2005); Bowker (2005).
85. Rhodes (2005).
86. Rhodes (2005).
87. Rhodes (2005).
88. Pew Forum on Religion and Public Life (2008).
89. Rhodes (2005); Bowker (2005).
90. Rhodes (2005).
91. Rhodes (2005).
92. Rhodes (2005).
93. Bowker (2005).
94. Rhodes (2005).
95. Pew Forum on Religion and Public Life (2008).
96. Pew Forum on Religion and Public Life (2008).
97. Bowker (2005).
98. Bowker (2005).
99. Bowker (2005).

100. Pew Forum on Religion and Public Life (2008).
101. Bowker (2005).
102. Bowker (2005).
103. Beverley (2009).
104. Beverley (2009).
105. Rhodes (2005).
106. Rhodes (2005).
107. Rhodes (2005).
108. Pew Forum on Religion and Public Life (2008).
109. Rhodes (2005).
110. Pew Forum (2011).
111. Rhodes (2005).
112. Rhodes (2005).
113. Oleksa (1992).
114. Hunt and Penwell (2008).
115. Hunt and Penwell (2008).
116. Bowker (2005).
117. Hunt and Penwell (2008).
118. Pew Forum on Religion and Public Life (2008).
119. Pew Forum on Religion and Public Life (2008).
120. Bowker (2005).
121. Hunt and Penwell (2008).
122. Hunt and Penwell (2008).
123. Hunt and Penwell (2008).
124. Hunt and Penwell (2008).
125. Hunt and Penwell (2008).
126. Hunt and Penwell (2008).
127. Hunt and Penwell (2008).
128. Alserhan (2010), pp. 34–49.
129. Hashim and Mizerski (2010), pp. 37–50.
130. Alserhan (2010), pp. 34–49; Hashim and Mizerski (2010), pp. 37–50.
131. Alserhan (2010), pp. 34–49.
132. Heiman, Just, McWilliams and Zilberman (2004), pp. 9–11.
133. Luqmani, Yavas and Quraeshi (1989), pp. 59–72.
134. Uddin (1997).
135. Hunt and Penwell (2008).
136. Hunt and Penwell (2008).
137. Cohen, Siegel and Rozin (2003), pp. 287–295.
138. Bowker (2005).
139. Pew Forum on Religion and Public Life (2008).
140. Hunt and Penwell (2008).
141. Hunt and Penwell (2008).

142. Hunt and Penwell (2008).
143. Hunt and Penwell (2008).
144. Hunt and Penwell (2008).
145. Hunt and Penwell (2008).
146. Hunt and Penwell (2008).
147. Hunt and Penwell (2008).
148. Hunt and Penwell (2008).
149. Alserhan (2010), pp. 34–49.
150. Severson (2010, January 10).
151. Diamond (2002), pp. 488–505.
152. Diamond (2002), pp. 488–505.
153. Heiman, Just, McWilliams and Zilberman (2004), pp. 9–11.
154. Shields (Producer) (2011).

Chapter 4

1. Bowker (2005).
2. Hunt and Penwell (2008).
3. Hunt and Penwell (2008).
4. Bowker (2005).
5. Bowker (2006).
6. Pew Forum on Religion and Public Life (2008).
7. Bowker (2006).
8. Hunt and Penwell (2008).
9. Hunt and Penwell (2008).
10. Smith (1991).
11. Smith (1991).
12. Buddha Dharma Education Association (2013).
13. Hunt and Penwell (2008).
14. Hunt and Penwell (2008).
15. Hunt and Penwell (2008).
16. Smith (1991).
17. Smith (1991).
18. Bowker (2005).
19. Bowker (2006).
20. Bowker (2006).
21. Hunt and Penwell (2008).
22. Hunt and Penwell (2008).
23. Hunt and Penwell (2008).
24. Pew Forum on Religion and Public Life (2008).
25. Bowker (2005); Hunt and Penwell (2008).

26. Bowker (2006).
27. Hunt and Penwell (2008).
28. Hunt and Penwell (2008).
29. Hunt and Penwell (2008).
30. Smith (1991).
31. Hinduism Today Magazine (2007).
32. Hunt and Penwell (2008).
33. Hunt and Penwell (2008).
34. Karoub (2013).
35. Hinduism Today Magazine (2007).
36. Bowker (2005); Bowker (2006).
37. Hunt and Penwell (2008).
38. Bowker (2006).
39. Bowker (2005).
40. Bowker (2005).
41. Bowker (2006).
42. Bowker (2005).
43. Bowker (2005).
44. Bowker (2006).
45. Bowker (2006).
46. Bowker (2006).
47. Hunt and Penwell (2008).
48. Central Intelligence Agency of the United States (2011).
49. McDermott (2008).
50. Smith (1991).
51. McDermott (2008).
52. Allison (2011).
53. McDermott (2008).
54. Smith (1991).
55. McDermott (2008).
56. McDermott (2008).
57. Smith (1991).
58. Smith (1991).

Chapter 5

1. Bennis (2013).
2. Bennis (2013).
3. Hirschman (1983), pp. 131–170; Lindridge (2005), pp. 142–151; Rindfleisch, Wong, and Burroughs (2010).
4. Choi, Kale, and Shin (2010), pp. 61–68.

5. Cutler (1991), pp. 153–164.
6. Delener (1994), pp. 36–53.
7. Hirschman (1983), pp. 131–170.
8. Iannaccone (1998), pp. 1465–1495.
9. Hirschman (1983), pp. 131–170; Kahle, Kau, Tambyah, Tan, and Jung (2005); LaBarbera and Gurhan (1997), pp. 71–97; Mokhlis (2006), pp. 64–74; Poria, Butler, and Airey (2003), pp. 340–363; Rindfleisch, Wong, and Burroughs (2010); Bailey and Sood (1993), pp. 328–352.
10. Hirschman (1983), pp. 131–170.
11. Al-Makaty, Van Tubergen, Whitlow and Boyd (1996), pp. 16–26.
12. Kahle, Kau, Tambyah, Tan, and Jung (2005).
13. Gross and Simmons (2009), pp. 101–129.
14. Gross and Simmons (2009), pp. 101–129.
15. Gross and Simmons (2009), pp. 101–129; Schuster and Finkelstein (2006).
16. Andeleeb (1993), pp. 42–49; Chandrasekaran and Tellis (2008), pp. 844–860; Delener (1994), pp. 36–53; Fam, Waller, and Erdogan (2004), pp. 537–555; Harrell (1986); Hirschman (1983), pp. 131–170; LaBarbera (1987), pp. 193–222; Oguinn and Belk (1989), pp. 227–238; Schiffman and Kanuk (2007); Sood and Nasu (1995), pp. 1–9; Bailey and Sood (1993), pp. 328–352.
17. Khraim (2010), pp. 166–179.
18. Mittelstaedt (2002), pp. 6–18.
19. Essoo and Dibb (2004), pp. 683–712; Hirschman (1981), pp. 102–110; Kahle, Kau, Tambyah, Tan, and Jung (2005); Wong and Burroughs (2010).
20. McDaniel and Burnett (1990), pp. 101–112.
21. Kahle, Kau, Tambyah, Tan and Jung (2005).

Chapter 6

1. Homer and Kahle (1988), pp. 638–646.
2. Kahle and Berman (1979); Homer and Kahle (1988), pp. 638–646; Kahle, Kulka, and Klingel (1980), pp. 492–502; Kahle (1984).
3. Engel (1976), pp. 98–101.
4. Thompson and Raine (1976), pp. 71–78.
5. Engel (1976), pp. 98–101.
6. Wilkes, Burnett and Howell (1986), pp. 47–56.
7. Hirschman (1981), pp. 102–110; Hirschman (1982), pp. 228–233; Hirschman (1983), pp. 131–170.
8. Bailey and Sood (1993), pp. 328–352.
9. Sood and Nasu (1995), pp. 1–9.

10. McDaniel and Burnett (1990), pp. 101–112; McDaniel and Burnett (1991), pp. 26–33.
11. LaBarbera (1987), pp. 193–222.
12. Delener (1990), pp. 27–38; Delener (1994), pp. 36–53.
13. Harrell (1986).
14. Mittelstaedt (2002), pp. 6–18.
15. Fam, Waller and Erdogan (2004), pp. 537–555.
16. Harrell (1986); Schiffman and Kanuk (2007); Solomon (2011).
17. Solomon (2011).
18. Thompson (2005).
19. Bhasin and Hicken (2012).
20. Rinallo, Scott and Maclaran (2012).
21. Kahle, Kau, Tambyah, Tan and Jung (2005).
22. Kahle, Kau, Tambyah, Tan and Jung (2005).
23. Kahle, Kau, Tambyah, Tan and Jung (2005).
24. Kahle, Kau, Tambyah, Tan and Jung (2005).
25. Hunt and Vitell (2006), pp. 1–11.
26. Hunt and Vitell (2006), pp. 1–11.
27. Clark and Dawson (1996), pp. 359–372; Cornwell et al. (2005), pp. 531–546.
28. Babakus, Cornwell, Mitchell and Schlegelmilch (2004), pp. 254–263.
29. Patwardhan, Keith and Vitell (2012), pp. 61–70.
30. Cornwell et al. (2005), pp. 531–546.
31. Babakus, Cornwell, Mitchell and Schlegelmilch (2004), pp. 254–263; Cornwell et al. (2005), pp. 531–546.
32. Fam, Waller and Erdogan (2004), pp. 537–555.
33. Putrevu and Swimberghek (2013), pp. 351–365.
34. Fam, Waller and Erdogan (2004), pp. 537–555.
35. Doran and Natale (2011), pp. 1–15.
36. Hirschman (1981), pp. 102–110; Hirschman (1982), pp. 228–233.
37. Hirschman (1982), pp. 228–233.
38. Hirschman (1982), pp. 228–233.
39. Mokhlis and Terengganu (2009), pp. 67–76.
40. Smidt et al. (2003), pp. 515–532.
41. Guiso, Sapienza and Zingales (2003), pp. 225–282.
42. Zaichkowsky and Sood (1989), pp. 20–34.
43. Mokhlis and Terengganu (2009), pp. 67–76.
44. Heiman, Just, McWilliams and Zilberman (2004), pp. 9–11.
45. Heiman, Just, McWilliams and Zilberman (2004), pp. 9–11.
46. Mokhlis and Terengganu (2009), pp. 67–76.
47. Mokhlis and Terengganu (2009), pp. 67–76.

48. Siguaw and Simpson (1997), pp. 23–40.
49. Sood and Nasu (1995), pp. 1–9.
50. Essoo and Dibb (2004), pp. 683–712.
51. Essoo and Dibb (2004), pp. 683–712.
52. Loroz (2006), pp. 308-309.
53. Speck and Peterson (2010), pp. 133–159.
54. Minton (2014).
55. Martin and Bateman (2013).
56. Poria, Butler and Airey (2003), pp. 340–363.
57. Poria, Butler and Airey (2003), pp. 340–363.
58. Poria, Butler and Airey (2003), pp. 340–363.
59. Poria, Butler and Airey (2003), pp. 340–363.
60. Rindfleisch, Burroughs and Wong (2005), pp. 153–154.
61. Rindfleisch, Wong and Burroughs (2010).
62. Shachar, Erdem, Cutright and Fitzsimons (2011).
63. Mokhlis and Terengganu (2009), pp. 67–76.
64. Delener (1990), pp. 27–38.
65. Delener (1994), pp. 36–53.
66. Essoo and Dibb (2004), pp. 683–712.
67. Wilkes, Burnett and Howell (1986), pp. 47–56.
68. Hossain and Onyango (2004), pp. 255–267.
69. Jianfeng, Hongping and Lanying (2009), pp. 31–34.
70. Muhamad and Mizerski (2007), pp. 74–85.
71. Allport and Ross (1967), pp. 432–443.
72. Mokhlis (2006), pp. 64–74.
73. Mokhlis (2006), pp. 64–74.
74. McDaniel and Burnett (1990), pp. 101–112.
75. Swimberghe, Sharma and Flurry (2009), pp. 340–347.
76. Choi (2010), pp. 157–171.
77. Choi, Paulraj and Shin (2013), pp. 262–280.
78. Siguaw and Simpson (1997), pp. 23–40.
79. Siguaw and Simpson (1997), pp. 23–40.
80. Siguaw and Simpson (1997), pp. 23–40.
81. Poria, Butler and Airey (2003), pp. 340–363.
82. LaBarbera and Gurhan (1997), pp. 71–97.
83. Rinallo, Scott and Maclaran (2012).
84. Speck and Roy. (2008).1197–1219.
85. McDaniel and Burnett (1990), pp. 101–112.
86. Zaichkowsky and Sood (1989), pp. 20–34.
87. Belk, Wallendorf and Sherry (1989), pp. 1–38.
88. Babakus, Cornwell, Mitchell and Schlegelmilch (2004), pp. 254–263; Muhamad and Mizerski (2007), pp. 74–85; Wilkes, Burnett, and Howell

(1986), pp. 47–56; Ong and Moschis (2006), pp. 1–13; Bailey and Sood (1993), pp. 328–352.

89. Bailey and Sood (1993), pp. 328–352.
90. Muhamad and Mizerski (2007), pp. 74–85.
91. Muhamad and Mizerski (2007), pp. 74–85.
92. Babakus, Cornwell, Mitchell and Schlegelmilch (2004), pp. 254–263; Bailey and Sood (1993), pp. 328–352.
93. Bailey and Sood (1993), pp. 328–352.
94. Wilkes, Burnett and Howell (1986), pp. 47–56.
95. Haley, White and Cunningham (2001); LaBarbera (1987), pp. 193–222; Rindfleisch, Wong and Burroughs (2010).
96. Haley, White and Cunningham (2001).
97. LaBarbera (1987), pp. 193–222.
98. LaBarbera (1987), pp. 193–222.
99. LaBarbera (1987), pp. 193–222.
100. Haley, White and Cunningham (2001).
101. Dotson and Hyatt (2000), pp. 63–68.
102. Henley Jr, Philhours, Ranganathan and Bush (2009), pp. 89–103.
103. Dotson and Hyatt (2000), pp. 63–68.
104. Taylor, Halstead and Haynes (2010), pp. 79–92.
105. Taylor, Halstead and Haynes (2010), pp. 79–92.
106. Taylor, Halstead and Haynes (2010), pp. 79–92.
107. Andeleeb (1993), pp. 42–49.
108. Belk, Wallendorf and Sherry (1989), pp. 1–38.
109. Belk, Wallendorf and Sherry (1989), pp. 1–38.
110. National Retail Foundation (2012).
111. Belk, Wallendorf and Sherry (1989), pp. 1–38.
112. Haley, White and Cunningham (2001).
113. Oguinn and Belk (1989), pp. 227–238.
114. Mittelstaedt (2002), pp. 6–18.
115. Einstein (2013).

Chapter 7

1. Azar (2010), pp. 52–56.
2. Emmons and Paloutzian (2003), pp. 377–402.
3. Emmons and Paloutzian (2003), pp. 377–402.
4. Emmons and Paloutzian (2003), pp. 377–402.
5. Emmons and Paloutzian (2003), pp. 377–402.
6. Zaidman, Goldstein and Nehemya (2009), pp. 597–621.
7. Piedmont (1999), pp. 985–1013; Rican and Janosova (2010), pp. 2–13.
8. Emmons and Paloutzian (2003), pp. 377–402.

9. Azar (2010), pp. 52–56.
10. Barton and Vaughan (1976), pp. 11–16.
11. Chamberlain and Zika (1988), pp. 411–420; LaBarbera and Gurhan (1997), pp. 71–97; Witter, Stock, Okun and Haring (1985), pp. 332–342.
12. Swinyard, Kau and Phua (2001), pp. 13–32.
13. Swinyard, Kau and Phua (2001), pp. 13–32.
14. Swinyard, Kau and Phua (2001), pp. 13–32.
15. Saroglou, Pichon, Trompette, Verschueren and Dernelle (2005), pp. 323–348.
16. Burroughs and Rindfleisch (2002), pp. 348–370.
17. McKee (2003).
18. Wiebe and Fleck (1980), pp. 181–187.
19. Wiebe and Fleck (1980), pp. 181–187.
20. Wiebe and Fleck (1980), pp. 181–187.
21. Mattila, Apostolopoulos, Sonmez, Yu and Sasidharan (2001), p. 193.
22. Bailey and Sood (1993), pp. 328–352.
23. Delener (1990), pp. 27–38.
24. Poulson, Eppler, Satterwhite, Wuensch and Bass (1998), pp. 227–232.
25. Vitell and Paolillo (2003), pp. 151–162.
26. Poulson, Eppler, Satterwhite, Wuensch and Bass (1998), pp. 227–232.
27. Kahle, Kau, Tambyah, Tan and Jung (2005).
28. Muniz and Schau (2005), pp. 737–747; Stark and Bainbridge (1980), pp. 1376–1395.
29. Weaver and Agle (2002), pp. 77–97.
30. Tajfel and Turner (1979), pp. 33–47.
31. Michon, Chebat and Kahle (2011).
32. Allport and Ross (1967), pp. 432–443.
33. Azar (2010), pp. 52–56.
34. Djupe (2000), pp. 78–89.
35. Lenski (1963).
36. Stark and Bainbridge (1980), pp. 1376–1395.
37. Choi, Kale and Shin (2010), pp. 61–68.
38. Cosgel and Minkler (2004), pp. 339–350.
39. Cosgel and Minkler (2004), pp. 339–350.
40. Greeley (1963), pp. 21–31.
41. Kahle, Kau, Tambyah, Tan and Jung (2005).
42. Kale (2004), pp. 92–107; Kahle and Valette (2012).
43. Helland (2002), pp. 293–302.
44. Wikipedia (2013).
45. Jaynes (2000).
46. Boyer (2001).

47. Adler and Jahn (1933).
48. Erikson (1958).
49. Fromm (1950).
50. James (1902/2004).
51. Allport (1950).
52. Pargament (2001).
53. Frankl (2011).
54. Maslow (1970).
55. Hood, Hill and Spilka (2009).
56. Kahle, Homer, O'Brien and Boush (1997), pp. 111–137.
57. Emmons and Paloutzian (2003), pp. 377–402.
58. Hood, Hill and Spilka (2009).

Chapter 8

1. Heiman, Just, McWilliams and Zilberman (2004), pp. 9–11.
2. Kale (2004), pp. 92–107.
3. Al-Makaty, Van, Whitlow and Boyd (1996), pp. 16–26; Al and Karande (2000), pp. 69–82; Luqmani, Yavas and Quraeshi (1989), pp. 59–72.
4. Alserhan (2010), pp. 34–49.
5. Al and Karande (2000), pp. 69–82.
6. Luqmani, Yavas and Quraeshi (1989), pp. 59–72.
7. Al and Karande (2000), pp. 69–82.
8. Muhamad and Mizerski (2007), pp. 74–85.
9. Muhamad and Mizerski (2010), pp. 124–135; Hashim and Mizerski (2010), pp. 37–50.
10. Hashim and Mizerski (2010), pp. 37–50.
11. Hashim and Mizerski (2010), pp. 37–50.
12. Luqmani, Yavas and Quraeshi (1989), pp. 59–72.
13. Al, Van, Whitlow and Boyd (1996), pp. 16–26.
14. Alserhan (2010), pp. 34–49.
15. Alserhan (2010), pp. 34–49.
16. Izberk (2013).
17. Alserhan (2010), pp. 34–49.
18. Diamond (2002), pp. 488–505.
19. Alserhan (2010), pp. 34–49.
20. Heiman, Just, McWilliams and Zilberman (2004), pp. 9–11.
21. Essoo and Dibb (2004), pp. 683–712; LaBarbera and Gurhan (1997), pp. 71–97; Loroz (2006), pp. 308–309; McKee (2003).
22. Mokhlis (2006), pp. 64–74.
23. Delener (1994), pp. 36–53.

24. McDaniel and Burnett (1990), pp. 101–112.
25. Engel (1976), pp. 98–101.
26. Fam, Waller and Erdogan (2004), pp. 537–555.
27. McDaniel and Burnett (1991), pp. 26–33.
28. Fam, Waller and Erdogan (2004), pp. 537–555.
29. Michell and Al (1999), pp. 427–444.
30. Wang (2013).
31. Choi, Kale and Shin (2010), pp. 61–68.
32. Chandrasekaran and Tellis (2008), pp. 844–860.

Chapter 9

1. Schneiderman (2011).
2. Zoll (2010),
3. BestBuy (2013).
4. FoxNews (2009).
5. Tackett (2013), pp. 26–27.
6. Dias (2013), pp. 20–28.
7. Deuze (2006), pp. 63–75.
8. Powers (2011).
9. McDonald, Oates, Young and Hwang (2006), pp. 515–534; Tanner and Wölfing (2003), pp. 883–902.
10. White (1967), pp. 1203–1207.
11. Eckberg and Blocker (1989), pp. 509–517.
12. Wolkomir, Futreal, Woodrum and Hoban (1997), pp. 325–343.
13. Corraliza and Berenguer (2000), pp. 832–848; Kollmuss and Agyeman (2002), pp. 239–260.
14. Granzin and Olsen (1991), pp. 1–27; Kollmuss and Agyeman (2002), pp. 239–260.
15. Johnson et al. (1989), pp. 855–868.
16. Bailey and Sood (1993), pp. 328–352; Fam, Waller and Erdogan (2004), pp. 537–555.
17. Homer and Kahle (1988), pp. 638–646.
18. Wilson (2012).
19. James (1902/2004).
20. Sarre (1995), pp. 115–127.
21. White (1967), pp. 1203–1207.
22. Hunt and Penwell (2008); Sarre (1995), pp. 115–127.
23. Minton, Lee, Orth, Kim and Kahle (2012), pp. 69–84.

References

Adler, A., & Jahn, E. (1933). *Religion and psychology*. Frankfurt, HE.

Allison, R. (2011). Confucianism and taoism. In L. Bouckaert & L. Zsolnia (Eds.), *The palgrave handbook of spirituality and business*. New York, NY: Palvgrave Macmillon.

Allport, G. W., & Ross, J. M. (1967). Personal religious orientation and prejudice. *Journal of Personality and Social Psychology 5*(4), 432–443.

Allport, G. W. (1950). *The individual and his religion: A psychological interpretation*. New York, NY: Macmillan.

Al-Makaty, S. S., Van Tubergen, G. N., Whitlow, S. S., & Boyd, D. A. (1996). Attitudes toward advertising in Islam. *Journal of Advertising Research 36*(3), 16–26.

Al-Olayan, F. S., & Karande, K. (2000). A content analysis of magazine advertisements from the United States and the Arab world. *Journal of Advertising 29*(3), 69–82.

Alserhan, B. A. (2010). Islamic branding: A conceptualization of related terms. *Journal of Brand Management 18*(1), 34–49.

Andeleeb, S. S. (1993). Religious affiliations and consumer behavior: An examination of hospitals. *Journal of Health Care Marketing 13*(4), 42–49.

Atwood, C. D. (2010). *Handbook of denominations in the United States* (XIIIth ed.). Nashville, TN: Abingdon Press.

Azar, B. (2010). A reason to believe. *American Psychology Association 41*(11), 52–56.

Babakus, E., Cornwell, T. B., Mitchell, V., & Schlegelmilch, B. (2004). Reactions to unethical consumer behavior across six countries. *Journal of Consumer Marketing 21*(4), 254–263.

Bailey, J. M., & Sood, J. (1993). The effects of religious affiliation on consumer behavior: A preliminary investigation. *Journal of Managerial Issues 5*(3), 328–352.

Barton, K., & Vaughan, G. M. (1976). Church membership and personality: A longitudinal-study. *Social Behavior and Personality 4*(1), 11–16.

Belk, R. W., Wallendorf, M., & Sherry, J. F. (1989). The sacred and the profane in consumer behavior: Theodicy on the odyssey. *Journal of Consumer Research 16*(1), 1–38.

Bennis, W. (2013). *Does religion belong in the b-school curriculum?* Retrieved April 25, 2013, from Businessweek: http://mobile.businessweek.com/articles/2013-01-22/does-religion-belong-in-the-b-school-curriculum

BestBuy (Producer). (2013). *About best buy.* Retrieved May 18, 2013, from http://pr.bby.com/about-best-buy/

Beverley, J. A. (2009). *Nelson's illustrated guide to religions.* Nashville, TN: Thomas Nelson Inc.

Bhasin, K., & Hicken, M. (2012). *17 Big companies that are intensely religious.* Retrieved January 19, 2012, from Business Insider: http://www.businessinsider.com/17-big-companies-that-are-intensely-religious-2012-1?op=1

Bowker, J. (2005). *The concise Oxford dictionary of world religions.* New York, NY: Oxford University Press.

Bowker, J. (2006). *World religions: The great faiths explored and explained.* New York, NY: Dorling Kindersley Limited.

Boyer, P. (2001). *Religion explained: The evolutionary origins of religious thought.* New York, NY: Basic books.

Buddha Dharma Education Association. (2013). *The buddhist schools: Theravada and mahayana.* Retrieved April 22, 2013, from http://www.buddhanet.net/e-learning/buddhistworld/schools1.htm

Burroughs, J. E., & Rindfleisch, A. (2002). Materialism and well-being: A conflicting values perspective. *Journal of Consumer Research 29*(3), 348–370.

Central Intelligence Agency of the United States. (2011). *CIA World Factbook.* Washington, DC: Central Intelligence Agency.

Chamberlain, K., & Zika, S. (1988). Religiosity, life meaning and wellbeing : some relationships in a sample of women. *Journal for the Scientific Study of Religion 27*(3), 411–420.

Chandrasekaran, D., & Tellis, G. J. (2008). Global takeoff of new products: Culture, wealth, or vanishing differences? *Marketing Science 27*(5), 844–860.

Choi, Y., Kale, R., & Shin, J. (2010). Religiosity and consumers' use of product information source among Korean consumers: An exploratory research. *International Journal of Consumer Studies 34*(1), 61–68.

Choi, Y., Paulraj, A., & Shin, J. (2013). Religion or religiosity: Which is the culprit for consumer switching behavior? *Journal of International Consumer Marketing 25*(4), 262–280.

Choi, Y., Kale, R., & Shin, J. (2010). Religiosity and consumers' use of product information source among Korean consumers: An exploratory research. *International Journal of Consumer Studies 34*(1), 61–68.

Choi, Y. (2010). Religion, religiosity, and South Korean consumer switching behaviors. *Journal of Consumer Behaviour 9*(3), 157–171.

Clark, J. W., & Dawson, L. E. (1996). Personal religiousness and ethical judgements: An empirical analysis. *Journal of Business Ethics 15*(3), 359–372.

Cohen, A. B., Siegel, J. I., & Rozin, P. (2003). Faith versus practice: Different bases for religiosity judgments by jews and protestants. *European Journal of Social Psychology 33*(2), 287–295.

Cornwell, B., Cui, C. C., Mitchell, V., Schlegelmilch, B., Dzulkiflee, A., & Chan, J. (2005). A cross-cultural study of the role of religion in consumers' ethical positions. *International Marketing Review 22*(5), 531–546.

Corraliza, J. A., & Berenguer, J. (2000). Environmental values, beliefs, and actions. *Environment and Behavior 32*(6), 832–848.

Cosgel, M. M., & Minkler, L. (2004). Religious identity and consumption. *Review of Social Economy 62*(3), 339–350.

Cutler, B. D. (1991). Religion and marketing: Important research area or a footnote in the literature? *Services Marketing Quarterly 8*(1), 153–164.

Dejong, G. F., Faulkner, J. E., & Warland, R. H. (1976). Dimensions of religiosity reconsidered: Evidence from a cross-cultural study. *Social Forces 54*(4), 866–889.

Delener, N. (1990). The effects of religious factors on perceived risk in durable goods purchase decisions. *Journal of Consumer Marketing 7*(3), 27–38.

Delener, N. (1994). Religious contrasts in consumer decision behaviour patterns: Their dimensions and marketing implications. *European Journal of Marketing 28*(5), 36–53.

Deuze, M. (2006). Participation, remediation, bricolage: Considering principal components of a digital culture. *The information society 22*(2), 63–75.

Diamond, E. (2002). The kosher lifestyle: Religious consumerism and suburban orthodox jews. *Journal of Urban History 28*(4), 488–505.

Dias, E. (2013, April 4). Evangelicos! *Time,* pp. 20–28.

Djupe, P. A. (2000). Religious brand loyalty and political loyalties. *Journal for the Scientific Study of Religion 39*(1), 78–89.

Donahue, M. J. (1985). Intrinsic and extrinsic religiousness: The empirical research. *Journal for the Scientific Study of Religion 24*(4), 418–423.

Doran, C. J., & Natale, S. M. (2011). Empatheia and caritas: The role of religion in fair trade consumption. *Journal of Business Ethics 98*(1), 1–15.

Dotson, M. J., & Hyatt, E. M. (2000). Religious symbols as peripheral cues in advertising: A replication of the elaboration likelihood model. *Journal of Business Research 48*(1), 63–68.

Eckberg, D. L., & Blocker, T. J. (1989). Varieties of Religious Involvement and Environmental Concerns: Testing the Lynn White Thesis. *Journal for the Scientific Study of Religion 28*(4), 509–517.

Einstein, M. (2013). Branding faith and managing reputations. In D. Rinallo, L. Scott and P. Maclaran (Eds.), *Consumption and spirituality*. New York, NY: Routledge

Emmons, R. A., & Paloutzian, R. F. (2003). The psychology of religion. *Annual Review of Psychology 54*(1), 377–402.

Engel, J. F. (1976). Psychographic research in a cross-cultural non product setting. *Advances in Consumer Research 3*, 98–101.

Erikson, E. H. (1958). *Young man Luther: A study in psychoanalysis and history*. New York, NY: WW Norton

Essoo, N., & Dibb, S. (2004). Religious influences on shopping behaviour: An exploratory study. *Journal of Marketing Management 20*(7), 683–712.

Evans, J. R., & Berman, B. (2010). *Marketing: Marketing in the 21st century* (XIth ed.). Mason, OH: Atomic Dog Publishing.

Fam, K. S., Waller, D. S., & Erdogan, B. Z. (2004). The influence of religion on attitudes towards the advertising of controversial products. *European Journal of Marketing 38*(5/6), 537–555.

Faulkner, J. E., & Dejong, G. F. (1966). Religiosity in 5-D: An empirical analysis. *Social Forces 45*(2), 246–254.

Forthun, L. F., Bell, N. J., Peek, C. W., & Sun, S. (1999). Religiosity, sensation seeking and alcohol/drug use in denominational and gender contexts. *Journal of Drug Issues 29*, 75–90.

FoxNews.com (Producer). (2009). *Best buy ad touting Muslim holiday sparks debate*. Retrieved May 18, 2013, from http://www.foxnews.com/story/2009/11/24/best-buy-ad-touting-muslim-holiday-sparks-debate/

Frankl, V. E. (2011). *Man's search for ultimate meaning*. New York, NY: Random House.

Fromm, E. (1950). *Psychoanalysis and religion*. New Haven, CT: Yale University Press.

Gay, D. A., & Lynxwiler, J. P. (2010). The impact of race and denominational variations in social attitudes: The issue and its dimensions. *Sociological Spectrum: Mid-South Sociological Association 30*(1), 110–127.

Granzin, K. L., & Olsen, J. E. (1991). Characterizing participants in activities protecting the environment: A focus on donating, recycling, and conservation behaviors. *Journal of Public Policy & Marketing 10*(2), 1–27.

Greeley, A. M. (1963). Note on the origins of religious differences. *Journal for the Scientific Study of Religion 3*(1), 21–31.

Gross, N., & Simmons, S. (2009). The religiosity of American college and university professors. *Sociology of Religion 70*(2), 101–129.

Guiso, L., Sapienza, P., & Zingales, L. (2003). People's opium? Religion and economic attitudes. *Journal of Monetary Economics 50*(1), 225–282.

Haley, E., White, C., & Cunningham, A. (2001). Branding religion: Christian consumers' understanding of Christian products. In J. M. Buddenbaum and D. A. Stout (Eds.), *Religion and popular culture: Studies on the interaction of worldviews*. Ames, IA: Iowa State University Press.

Harrell, G. D. (1986). *Consumer behavior*. San Diego, CA: Harcourt Brace Jovanovich

Hashim, N. M., & Mizerski, D. (2010). Exploring Muslim consumers' information sources for fatwa rulings on products and behaviors. *Journal of Islamic Marketing 1*(1), 37–50.

Heiman, A., Just, D., McWilliams,B., & Zilberman, D. (2004). Religion, religiosity, and food consumption. *Journal of Food Quality and Preferences 8*, 9–11.

Helland, C. (2002). Surfing for salvation. *Religion 32*(4), 293–302.

Henley Jr, W. H., Philhours, M. P., Ranganathan, S. K., & Bush, A. J. (2009). The effects of symbol product relevance and religiosity on consumer perceptions of Christian symbols in advertising. *Journal of Current Issues and Research in Advertising 31*(1), 89–103.

Hill, P. C., & Hood, R. W. (1999). *Measures of religiosity.* Birmingham, AL: Religious Education Press.

Hill, P. C., Pargament, K., Hood, R. W., McCullough, M. E., Swyers, J. P., Larson, D. B., & Zinnbauer, B. J. (2000). Conceptualizing religion and spirituality: Points of commonality, points of departure. *Journal for the Theory of Social Behaviour 30*(1), 51–77.

Himmelfarb, H. S. (1975). Measuring religious involvement. *Social Forces 53*(4), 606–618.

Hinduism Today Magazine. (2007). *What is Hinduism? Modern adventures into a profound global faith.* Kapaa, HI: Himalayan Academy.

Hirschman, E. C. (1981). American jewish ethnicity: Its relationship to some selected aspects of consumer behavior. Journal of Marketing *45*(3), 102–110.

Hirschman, E. C. (1982). Religious differences in cognitions regarding novelty seeking and information transfer. *Advances in Consumer Research 10*, 228–233.

Hirschman, E. C. (1983). Religious affiliation and consumption processes: An initial paradigm. *Research in Marketing 6*, 131–170.

Hoffmann, J. P., & Miller, A. S. (1998). Denominational influences on socially divisive issues: Polarization or continuity? *Journal for the Scientific Study of Religion 37*(3), 528–546.

Hofstede, G. (1994). Management scientists are human. *Management Science 40*(1), 4–13.

Homer, P. M., & Kahle, L. R. (1988). A structural equation test of the value-attitude-behavior hierarchy. *Journal of Personality and Social Psychology 54*(4), 638–646.

Hood, R. W., Hill, P. C., & Spilka, B. (2009). *The psychology of religion: An empirical approach* (IVth ed.). New York, NY: The Guilford Press.

Hossain, F., & Onyango, B. (2004). Product attributes and consumer acceptance of nutritionally enhanced genetically modified foods. *International Journal of Consumer Studies 28*(3), 255–267.

Hunt, S. D., & Vitell, S. J. (2006). A general theory of marketing ethics: A revision and three questions. *Journal of Macromarketing 26*(2), 1–11.

Hunt, J., & Penwell, D. (2008). *AMG's handi-reference world religions and cults.* Chattanooga, TN: AMG Publishers.

Iannaccone, L. R. (1998). Introduction to the economics of religion. *Journal of Economic Literature 36*(3), 1465–1495.

Izberk-Bilgin, E. (2013). Theology meets the marketplace: The discurvsive formation of the *halal* market in Turkey. In D. Rinallo, L. Scott & P. Maclaran (Eds.), *Consumption and spirituality.* New York, NY: Routledge.

James, W. (1902/2004). *The varieties of religious experience.* New York, NY: Touchstone.

Jaynes, J. (2000). *The origin of consciousness in the breakdown of the bicameral mind.* Boston, MA: Houghton Mifflin Harcourt.

Jianfeng, Li., Hongping, Liu., & Lanying, Du. (2009). The effect of religiosity on shopping behavior: An exploratory study during the transitional period in China. *International Conference on Information Management, Innovation Management and Industrial Engineering 2*, pp. 31–34.

Johnson et al. (1989). Cross-cultural assessment of altruism and its correlates. *Personality and Individual Differences 10*(8), 855–868.

Johnstone-Louis, M. (2013). No gods. No masters? The "new atheist" movement and the commercialization of unbelief. In D. Rinallo, L. Scott and P. Maclaran (Eds.). *Consumption and spirituality.* New York, NY: Routledge.

Kahle, L. R., & Berman, J. J. (1979). Attitudes cause behaviors: A cross-lagged panel analysis. *Journal of Personality and Social Psychology 37*(3), 315–321.

Kahle, L. R., & Valette-Florence, P. (2012). *Marketplace lifestyles in an age of social media.* Armonk, NY: M.E. Sharpe Inc.

Kahle, L. R., Homer, P. M., O'Brien, R. M., & Boush, D. M. (1997). Maslow's hierarchy and social adaptation as alternative accounts of value structures In *Values, lifestyles and psychographics* (pp. 111–137). Mahway, NJ: Lawrence Erlbaum Associates.

Kahle, L. R., Kau, A., Tambyah, S., Tan, S., & Jung, K. (2005). Religion, religiosity, and values: Implications for consumer behavior. *Australian and New Zealand Marketing Academy Conference.*

Kahle, L. R., Kulka, R. A., & Klingel, D. M. (1980). Low adolescent self-esteem leads to multiple interpersonal problems: A test of social-adaptation theory. *Journal of Personality and Social Psychology 39*(3), 492–502.

Kahle, L. R. (1983). *Social values and social change: Adaptation to life in America.* New York, NY: Praeger.

Kahle, L. R. (1996). Social values and consumer behavior: Research from the list of values. In C. Seligman, J. M. Olson and M. P. Zanna (Eds.), *The psychology of values: The Ontario Symposium* (Vol. 8). Mahwah, NJ: Lawrence Erlbaum Associates.

Kahle, L. R., & Valette-Florence, P. (2012). *Marketplace lifestyles in an age of social media.* Armonk, NY: M.E. Sharpe Inc.

Kahle, L. R., Beatty, S. E., & Homer, P. (1986). Alternative measurement approaches to consumer values: The list of values (LOV) and values and life style (VALS). *Journal of Consumer Research 13*(3), 405–409.

Kahle, L. R., Rose, G. M., & Shoham, A. (2000). Findings of LOV throughout the world, and other evidence of cross-national consumer psychographics: Introduction. *Journal of Euromarketing 8*(1–2), 1–13.

Kahle, L. R. (1984). *Attitudes and social adaptation: A person-situation interaction approach.* Oxford, UK: Pergamon Press.

Kale, S. H. (2004). Spirituality, religion, and globalization. *Journal of Macromarketing, 24*(2), 92–107.

Karoub, J. (2013). *McDonald's settles suit over Islamic diet rules.* Retrieved January 21, 2013, from http://www.usatoday.com/story/money/business/2013/01/21/mcdonalds-islamic-diet-lawsuit/1852147/

Khraim, H. (2010). Measuring religiosity in consumer research from Islamic perspective. *International Journal of Marketing Studies 2*(2), 166–179.

King, M. B. (1967). Measuring the religious variable: 9 proposed dimensions. *Journal for the Scientific Study of Religion 6*(2), 173–190.

King, M. B., & Hunt, R. A. (1969). Measuring the religious variable: Amended findings. *Journal for the Scientific Study of Religion 8*(2), 321–323.

King, M. B., & Hunt, R. A. (1972). Measuring the religious variable: Replication. *Journal for the Scientific Study of Religion 11*(3), 240–251.

King, M. B., & Hunt, R. A. (1990). Measuring the religious variable: Final comment. *Journal for the Scientific Study of Religion 29*(4), 531–535.

Kollmuss, A., & Agyeman, J. (2002). Mind the gap: Why do people act environmentally and what are the barriers to pro-environmental behavior? *Environmental Education Research 8*(3), 239–260.

LaBarbera, P. A. & Gurhan, Z. (1997). The role of materialism, religiosity, and demographics in subjective well-being. *Psychology & Marketing 14*(1), 71–97.

LaBarbera, P. A. (1987). Consumer behavior and born again Christianity. *Research in Consumer Behavior 2*, 193–222.

Lenski, G. (1963). *The religious factor: A sociological study of religion's impact on politics, economics, and family life.* New York, NY: Doubleday.

Lindridge, A. (2005). Religiosity and the construction of a cultural-consumption identity. *Journal of Consumer Marketing 22*(3), 142–151.

Loroz, P. S. (2006). The generation gap: A Baby Boomer vs. Gen Y comparison of religiosity, consumer values, and advertising appeal effectiveness. *Advances in Consumer Research 33*(1), 308–309.

Luqmani, M., Yavas, U., & Quraeshi, Z. (1989). Advertising in Saudi Arabia: Content and regulation. *International Marketing Review 6*(1), 59–72.

Martin, W. C., & Bateman, C. R. (2013). Consumer religious commitment's influence on ecocentric attitudes and behavior. *Journal of Business Research in press.*

Maslow, A. H. (1970). *Religions, values, and peak-experiences.* New York, NY: Penguin.

Mattila, A. S., Apostolopoulos, Y., Sonmez, S., Yu, L., & Sasidharan, V. (2001). The impact of gender and religion on college students' spring break behavior. *Journal of Travel Research 40*(2), 193.

McDaniel, S. W., & Burnett, J. J. (1990). Consumer religiosity and retail store evaluative criteria. *Journal of the Academy of Marketing Science 18*(2), 101–112.

McDaniel, S. W., & Burnett, J. J. (1991). Targeting the evangelical market segment. *Journal of Advertising Research 31*(4), 26–33.

McDermott, G. R. (2008). *The Baker pocket guide to world religions.* Grand Rapids, MI: Baker Publishing Group.

McDonald, S., Oates, C. J., Young, C. W., & Hwang, K. (2006). Toward sustainable consumption: Researching voluntary simplifiers. *Psychology & Marketing 23*(6), 515–534.

McKee, D. (2003). Spirituality and marketing: An overview of the literature. In R. A. Giacalone and C. L. Jurkiewicz (Eds.), *Handbook of workplace spirituality and organizational performance.* Armonk, NY: ME Sharpe Inc.

Merriam-Webster. (2013). *Dictionary.* Retrieved August 15, 2013, from http://www.merriam-webster.com/dictionary/belief

Michell, P., & Al-Mossawi, M. (1999). Religious commitment related to message contentiousness. *International Journal of Advertising 18*(4), 427–444.

Michon, R., Chebat, J., & Kahle, L. R. (2011). Selling brotherhood to North-American multicultural markets: How life values mediate charitable donation behaviors. In J. Lengler and C. Mello (Eds.), *Personal values and strategic marketing.* Santa Cruz: doSul: EDUNISC (in print)

Minton, E., Lee, C., Orth, U., Kim, C., & Kahle, L. (2012). Sustainable marketing and social media: A cross-country analysis of motives for sustainable behaviors. *Journal of Advertising 41*(4), 69–84.

Minton, E. (2014). Religion and religiosity's influence on sustainable consumption behaviors. In L. R. Kahle and E. Gurel-Atay (Eds.), *Communicating sustainability for the green economy.* Armonk, NY: M.E.

Mittelstaedt, J. D. (2002). A framework for understanding the relationships between religions and markets. *Journal of Macromarketing 22*(1), 6–18.

Mokhlis, S. (2009). Religious differences in some selected aspects of consumer behaviour: A Malaysian study. *Journal of International Management 4*(1), 67–76.

Mokhlis, S. (2006). The effect of religiosity on shopping orientation: An exploratory study in Malaysia. *Journal of American Academy of Business 9*, 64–74.

Muhamad, N., & Mizerski, D. (2007). Muslim religious commitment related to intention to purchase taboo products. *Journal of Business and Policy Research* 3(1), 74–85.

Muhamad, N., & Mizerski, D. (2010). The constructs mediating religions' influence on buyers and consumers. *Journal of Islamic Marketing 1*(2), 124–135.

Muniz, A. M., & Schau, H. J. (2005). Religiosity in the abandoned Apple Newton brand community. *Journal of Consumer Research 31*(4), 737–747.

National Retail Foundation. (2012). *NFR's 2012 holiday survival kit*. In Federation (Ed.). Washington, DC: NRF.

New Strategist Publications. (2010). *American attitudes: Who thinks what about the issues that shape our lives* (VIth ed.). Ithaca, NY: New Strategist Publications Inc.

Nicolaievsky, B., & Maenchen, H. M. (1976). *Karl marx: Man and fighter*. New York, NY: Penguin Books.

Oguinn, T. C., & Belk, R. W. (1989). Heaven on Earth: Consumption at Heritage Village, USA. *Journal of Consumer Research 16*(2), 227–238.

Oleksa, M. J. (1992). *Orthodox Alaska: A theology of mission*. Yonkers, NY: St Vladimirs Seminary Press.

Ong, F. S., & Moschis, G. P. (2006). Religiosity and consumer behavior: A cross-cultural study *International Conference on Business and Information 3*, 1–13.

Pargament, K. I. (2001). *The psychology of religion and coping: Theory, research, practice*. New York, NY: Guilford Press.

Patwardhan, A. M., Keith, M. E., & Vitell, S. J. (2012). Religiosity, attitude toward business, and ethical beliefs: Hispanic consumers in the United States. *Journal of Business Ethics 110*(1), 61–70.

Pew Forum on Religion and Public Life. (2008). *U.S. religious landscape survey*. Washington, DC: Pew Research Center.

Piedmont, R. L. (1999). Does spirituality represent the sixth factor of personality? Spiritual transcendence and the five-factor model. *Journal of Personality 67*(6), 985–1013.

Poria, Y., Butler, R., & Airey, D. (2003). Tourism, religion and religiosity: A holy mess. *Current Issues in Tourism* 6(4), 340–363.

Poulson, R. L., Eppler, M. A., Satterwhite, T. N., Wuensch, K. L., & Bass, L. A. (1998). Alcohol consumption, strength of religious beliefs, and risky sexual behavior in college students. *Journal of American College Health 46*(5), 227–232.

Powers, D. (2011). The end of new music? Digital media, history, and the idea of attention. In D. Park, N. Jankowski and S. Jones (Eds.), *The long history of new media: Technology, historiography, and contextualizing newness*. New York, NY: Peter Lang Publishers.

Putrevu, S., & Swimberghek, K. (2013). The influence of religiosity on consumer ethical judgments and responses toward sexual appeals. *Journal of Business Ethics 115*(2), 351–365.

Reynolds, T. J., & Olson, J. C. (2001). *Understanding consumer decision making: The means-end approach to marketing and advertising strategy.* Mahwah, NJ: Psychology Press.

Rhodes, R. (2005). *The complete guide to Christian denominations.* Irvin, CA: Harvest House Pub.

Rican, P., & Janosova, P. (2010). Spirituality as a basic aspect of personality: A cross-cultural verification of Piedmont's model. *International Journal for the Psychology of Religion 20*(1), 2–13.

Rinallo, D., Scott, L., & Maclaran, P. (2012). *Consumption and Spirituality.* New York, NY: Routledge.

Rindfleisch, A., Burroughs, J. E., & Wong, N. (2005). Religiosity and brand commitment: A multicultural perspective. *Asia Pacific Advances in Consumer Research, 6,* 153–154.

Rindfleisch, A., Wong, N., & Burroughs, J. E. (2010). God & Mammon: The influence of religiosity on brand connections. In S. H. K. Wuyts, M. G. Dekimpe, E. Gijsbrecths and F. G. M. Pieters (Eds.), *The connected customer: The changing nature of consumer and business markets.* Mahwah, NJ: Lawrence-Erlbaum.

Saroglou, V., Pichon, I., Trompette, L., Verschueren, M., & Dernelle, R. (2005). Prosocial behavior and religion: New evidence based on projective measures and peer ratings. *Journal for the Scientific Study of Religion 44*(3), 323–348.

Sarre, P. (1995). Towards global environmental values: lessons from Western and Eastern experience. *Environmental Values 4*(2), 115–127.

Schiffman, L., & Kanuk, L. (2007). *Consumer behavior* (9th ed.). Upper Saddle River, NJ: Pearson Prentice Hall.

Schneiderman, D. (2013). *Best Buy ad's mention of Muslim holiday irks some consumers.* Retrieved May 18, 2013, from Huffington Post: http://www.huffingtonpost.com/2009/11/25/best-buy-flyers-muslim-ho_n_369583.html

Schuster, J., & Finkelstein, M. J. (2006). *The American faculty.* Baltimore, MD: Johns Hopkins University Press.

Seidlitz, L., Abernethy, A. D., Duberstein, P. R., Evinger, J. S., Chang, T. H., & Lewis, B. L. (2002). Development of the spiritual transcendence index. *Journal for the Scientific Study of Religion 41*(3), 439–453.

Severson, K. (2010). *For some, kosher equals pure.* Retrieved January 10, 2010, from New York Times: http://www.nytimes.com/2010/01/13/dining/13kosh.html?pagewanted=all&_r=1&

Shachar, R., Erdem, T., Cutright, K. C., & Fitzsimons, G. J. (2011). Brands: The opiate of the nonreligious masses? *Marketing Science 30*(1), 1–19.

Sherif, M. (1935). A study of some social factors in perception. *Archives of Psychology 27*(187), 23–46.

Shields, M. (2011). *What, a jewish groupon?.* Retrieved January 14, 2011, from Adweek: http://www.adweek.com/news/technology/what-jewish-groupon-125406

Siguaw, J. A., & Simpson, P. M. (1997). Effects of religiousness on Sunday shopping and outshopping behaviours: A study of shopper attitudes and behaviours in the American South. *The International Review of Retail, Distribution and Consumer Research 7*(1), 23–40.

Smidt et al. (2003). The political attitudes and activities of mainline Protestant clergy in the election of 2000: A study of six denominations. *Journal for the Scientific Study of Religion 42*(4), 515–532.

Smith, H. (1991). *The world's religions*. New York, NY: HarperOne.

Smith, T. W. (1990). Classifying protestant denominations. *Review of Religious Research 31*(3), 225–245.

Solomon, M. R. (2011). *Consumer behavior: Buying, having, and being* (9th ed.). Boston, MA: Prentice Hall.

Sood, J., & Nasu, Y. (1995). Religiosity and nationality: An exploratory study of their effect on consumer behavior in Japan and the United States. *Journal of Business Research 34*(1), 1–9.

Speck, S. K. S., & Peterson, T. (2010). Socialization of adult and young consumers into materialism: The roles of media and church in Peru. In R. W. Belk (Ed.), *Research in Consumer Behavior* (Vol. 12, pp. 133–159). Bingley, UK: Emerald Group Publishing Limited.

Speck, S. K. S., & Roy, A. (2008). The interrelationships between television viewing, values and perceived well-being: A global perspective. *Journal of International Business Studies 39*(7), 1197–1219.

Stabile, D. R. (2007). *Economics, competition and academia: An intellectual history of sophism versus virtue*. Northampton, MA: Edward Elgar Publishing.

Stark, R., & Bainbridge, W. S. (1980). Networks of faith: Interpersonal bonds and recruitment to cults and sects. *The American Journal of Sociology 85*(6), 1376–1395.

Sullivan, L. E. (2009). *The SAGE glossary of the social and behavioral sciences*. Thousand Oaks, CA: SAGE Publications, Incorporated.

Swimberghe, K., Sharma, D., & Flurry, L. (2009). An exploratory investigation of the consumer religious commitment and its influence on store loyalty and consumer complaint intentions. *Journal of Consumer Marketing 26*(5), 340–347.

Swinyard, W. R., Kau, A., & Phua, H. (2001). Happiness, materialism, and religious experience in the US and Singapore. *Journal of Happiness Studies 2*(1), 13–32.

Tackett, M. (2013, April). The democratic plot to take Texas. *Bloomberg Businessweek* 26–27.

Tajfel, H., & Turner, J. C. (1979). An integrative theory of intergroup conflict *The social psychology of intergroup relations 33*, 33–47.

Tanner, C., & Kast, S. W. (2003). Promoting sustainable consumption: Determinants of green purchases by Swiss consumers. *Psychology and Marketing 20*(10), 883–902.

Taylor, C. (2007). *A secular age*. Cambridge, MA: Harvard University Press.

Taylor, V. A., Halstead, D., & Haynes, P. J. (2010). Consumer responses to Christian religious symbols in advertising. *Journal of Advertising 39*(2), 79–92.

Thompson, S. (2005). *Fowl pray: Tyson gets religion*. Retrieved December 5, 2005, from http://adage.com/article/news/fowl-pray-tyson-religion/105444/

Thompson, H. A., & Raine, J. E. (1976). Religious denomination preference as a basis for store location. *Journal of Retailing 52*(2), 71–78.

Uddin, Z. (1997). *A handbook of halaal and haraam products*. New York, NY: Center for American Muslim Research and Information.

Vitell, J. S., & Paolillo, J. G. P. (2003). Consumer ethics: The role of religiosity. *Journal of Business Ethics 46*(2), 151–162.

Wang, Z. (2013). The influence of religion on perceptions toward regulations of controversial advertising *School of Management* (Vol. Masters of Science in Management). Lethbridge, CA: University of Lethbridge.

Weaver, G. R., & Agle, B. R. (2002). Religiosity and ethical behavior in organizations: A symbolic interactionist perspective. *Academy of Management Review 27*(1), 77–97.

White, L. (1967). The historical roots of our environmental crisis. *Science 155*(3767), 1203–1207.

Wiebe, K. F., & Fleck, J. R. (1980). Personality correlates of intrinsic, extrinsic, and non-religious orientations. *Journal of Psychology 105*(2), 181–187.

Wikipedia. (2013). *Psychology of religion*. Retrieved September 9, 2013, from en.wikipedia.org/wiki/Psychology_of_religion

Wilde, A., & Joseph, S. (1997). Religiosity and personality in a Moslem context. *Personality and Individual Differences 23*(5), 899–900

Wilkes, R. E., Burnett, J. J., & Howell, R. D. (1986). On the meaning and measurement of religiosity in consumer research. *Journal of the Academy of Marketing Science 14*(1), 47–56.

Wilson, L. (2012). *Churches Embrace the Genesis Covenant, Seek Greenfaith Certification*. Retrieved May 31, 2012, from Episcopal News Service: http://episcopaldigitalnetwork.com/ens/2012/05/31/churches-embrace-the-genesis-covenant-seek-greenfaith-certification/

Witter, R. A., Stock, W. A., Okun, M. A., & Haring, M. J. (1985). Religion and subjective well-being in adulthood: A quantitative synthesis. *Review of Religious Research 26*(4), 332–342.

Wolkomir, M., Futreal, M., Woodrum, E., & Hoban, T. (1997). Denominational subcultures of environmentalism. *Review of Religious Research 38*(4), 325–343.

Woodrum, E., & Wolkomir, M. J. (1997). Religious effects on environmentalism. *Sociological Spectrum: Mid-South Sociological Association 17*(2), 223–234.

Zaichkowsky, J. L., & Sood, J. H. (1989). A global look at consumer involvement and use of products. *International Marketing Review 6*(1), 20–34.

Zaidman, N., Goldstein-Gidoni, O., & Nehemya, I. (2009). From temples to organizations: The introduction and packaging of spirituality. *Organization 16*(4), 597–621.

Zinnbauer et al. (1997). Religion and spirituality : Unfuzzying the fuzzy. *Journal for the Scientific Study of Religion 36*(4), 549–564.

Zoll, R. *U.S. Muslims: A new consumer niche.* Retrieved December 28, 2010, from USA Today: http://usatoday30.usatoday.com/news/religion/2010-12-27-Muslim-consumers27_ST_N.htm

Index

Adventists, 33
Anglicans and Episcopalians, 32
Baptists, 29
Catholic-adherents, 27
C&E Christians, 14
Congregationalists, 33
Holiness, 32
household religious affiliation, 4
Latino Catholics, 28
Lutherans, 30
Methodists, 29–30
Mormons/Latter-Day Saints (LDS), 34
Muslims, 38–39
non-denominational adherents, 30
Pentecostals, 30
Presbyterians, 31
Protestants, 28

religious Americans, 4
Restorationists, 31
self-report praying, 4
Sunday Christians, 14
unaffiliated with any religious beliefs, 4

V
Vaishnavism, 48
Vaishyas, 48
Values, 9–10, 60, 78
Varieties of Religious Experience, 81

W
The Watchtower creed, 35
Wesley, J., 29
Wilkes, R.E., 12, 17
worship of nature, 10

OTHER TITLES IN ECONOMICS COLLECTION

Philip Romero, The University of Oregon and Jeffrey Edwards,
North Carolina A&T State University, Editors

- *Managerial Economics: Concepts and Principles* by Donald Stengel
- *Your Macroeconomic Edge: Investing Strategies for the Post-Recession World* by Philip J. Romero
- *Working with Economic Indicators: Interpretation and Sources* by Donald Stengel
- *Innovative Pricing Strategies to Increase Profits* by Daniel Marburger
- *Regression for Economics* by Shahdad Naghshpour
- *Statistics for Economics* by Shahdad Naghshpour
- *How Strong Is Your Firm's Competitive Advantage?* by Daniel Marburger
- *A Primer on Microeconomics* by Thomas Beveridge
- *Game Theory: Anticipating Reactions for Winning Actions* by Mark L. Burkey
- *A Primer on Macroeconomics* by Thomas Beveridge
- *Economic Decision Making Using Cost Data: A Guide for Managers* by Daniel Marburger
- *The Fundamentals of Money and Financial Systems* by Shahdad Naghshpour
- *International Economics: Understanding the Forces of Globalization for Managers* by Paul Torelli
- *The Economics of Crime* by Zagros Madjd-Sadjadi
- *Money and Banking: An Intermediate Market-Based Approach* by William D. Gerdes

Announcing the Business Expert Press Digital Library

*Concise E-books Business Students Need
for Classroom and Research*

This book can also be purchased in an e-book collection by your library as
- a one-time purchase,
- that is owned forever,
- allows for simultaneous readers,
- has no restrictions on printing, and
- can be downloaded as PDFs from within the library community.

Our digital library collections are a great solution to beat the rising cost of textbooks. e-books can be loaded into their course management systems or onto student's e-book readers.

The **Business Expert Press** digital libraries are very affordable, with no obligation to buy in future years. For more information, please visit **www.businessexpertpress.com/librarians**. To set up a trial in the United States, please contact **Adam Chesler** at *adam.chesler@ businessexpertpress.com* for all other regions, contact **Nicole Lee** at *nicole.lee@igroupnet.com*.

CPSIA information can be obtained at www.ICGtesting.com
Printed in the USA
BVOW11s1558091213

338502BV00004B/13/P